BEFORE THE FIELDS OF CROSSES

THE REMINISCENCES OF A SON ABOUT THE EXPLOITS OF HIS FATHER AT THE OUTBREAK OF WORLD WAR II

LOUIS RENSHAW FORTIER
With CHIP FORTIER

Printed in Victoria, Canada

National Library of Canada Cataloguing in Publication Data

Fortier, Louis Renshaw, 1924-
    Before the fields of crosses / Louis Renshaw Fortier, author ; Chip
Fortier, co-writer and editor.
Includes bibliographical references.
ISBN 1-4120-0046-7
    I. Fortier, Chip, 1955- II. Title.
D811.F67 2003   940.54'21971   C2003-901370-7

TRAFFORD

This book was published *on-demand* in cooperation with Trafford Publishing.
On-demand publishing is a unique process and service of making a book available for retail sale to the public taking advantage of on-demand manufacturing and Internet marketing.
On-demand publishing includes promotions, retail sales, manufacturing, order fulfilment, accounting and collecting royalties on behalf of the author.

Suite 6E, 2333 Government St., Victoria, B.C. V8T 4P4, CANADA
Phone   250-383-6864   Toll-free   1-888-232-4444 (Canada & US)
Fax   250-383-6804   E-mail   sales@trafford.com
Web site   www.trafford.com   TRAFFORD PUBLISHING IS A DIVISION OF TRAFFORD HOLDINGS LTD.
Trafford Catalogue #03-0409   www.trafford.com/robots/03-0409.html

10   9   8   7   6   5   4   3   2

BEFORE THE FIELDS OF CROSSES
(A Personal Memoir of a Memorable Era)

PREFACE:

This is the story of a father and son at the outbreak of World War II, before the millions of casualties of that war created the many *fields of crosses* that exist today. It relates some of the minor vignettes of life during those interesting years of this country's existence. The history books will recall the major events of that time, but hundreds of personal stories of the millions of people in Europe and the US who lived through those years will be lost to antiquity. Perhaps it is just as well. However, there are many people who would like to trace their heritage and who occasionally wonder what their grandparents or great-grandparents did during this World War II era. Perhaps this might be true of my own grandchildren; if so, this story is for them.

I am deeply indebted to my beloved wife, Peggy, for persuading me to stop telling these vignettes around the dining room table and to commit them to paper instead. I hope she approves of this effort. Without her enthusiastic and persistent effort I am afraid these stories would have died with me.

I would also like to acknowledge the contributions of my son, Chip; the son who bears his grandfather's name of Louis Joseph Fortier, II. His major role was to insure that all the facts presented were indeed verified.

The Twentieth Century closed as a period of momentous changes in the human condition. It was the American Century; the century in which the United States reached its zenith of power, and in doing so initiated vast and unprecedented changes that will affect all future generations: air travel, space exploration including man's landing on the moon, medical breakthroughs, and the information age. The middle of the century was an exciting time for a son to grow up in admiration of his father during some of the era's most tumultuous events.

In the Prologue, hopefully I have reduced the epoch history of the ten-year period of 1936-1945 to something that is meaningful. So vast a human endeavor as World War II does not lend itself to a simple and condensed format. I have not tried to relate the impact of this war on the second half of this century; nor have I introduced the next great "war" that followed which we know today as the "cold war" between the US and the USSR.

While this is primarily the story of my father, a few incidents of my Mother's fascinating life are included. Successful service wives are a special breed. They know loneliness, continual shift of residences, constant changing of schools and cultures in which their children are raised, and long periods when they are left alone to take care of the household while their spouses are serving their country. As you will see in this narrative they often share some of the dangers of that service. The first person to urge me to write my recollections was Mrs. Ruth Lawson, an Army wife, who kept insisting that we record some of the era in which we lived. Unfortunately, she did not write her own memoirs that would have included her and her daughter being strafed by Japanese planes on December 7, 1941. Hence in a sense I dedicate this treatise to all those ladies who backed their husbands during those very perilous times; particularly my Mother, my wonderful first wife Maureen, and my best pal and younger sister Margot.

I cannot enumerate the list of all the friends and family who helped me to put together this chronology, or kept me dedicated and on course while I was writing it. I am indebted to them far beyond my ability to thank them. They, of course, know who they are so let me recognize them collectively and once again tell them how much I appreciate their help; I could not have put this together without them. In saying this I also would like to make it clear that I, and I alone, am responsible for any errors of content or misstatements of fact.

These reminisces are mine alone. Others may have seen the situation differently, or remembered events more clearly than I did. Certainly my two sisters, who lived through these times with me, may have a different perception or memory of these specific times and events, but I know they share with me our great admiration for both my Mother and Father and the heritage these two parents passed down to their children and grandchildren. Ultimately all we receive is a gift from our Creator. I thank God for my Mother and Father's survival during these fateful events and dedicate this grandchildren's legacy to His greater glory.

Virginia Beach, VA   Louis Renshaw Fortier

September, 2002

INDEX

This story is of the period 1936-1945, which saw a junior Army captain emerge as a crack intelligence officer and commander of an Infantry Division; a small pre-teen boy grow up in unusual circumstances and himself become an army officer, and see the United States of America go from an isolationist country protected by its two ocean frontiers to a country that created fleets of ships, armadas of aircraft, and armies of millions of soldiers and projected them throughout the entire world.

Inasmuch as World War II began in the 1930s, most people today have only a vague knowledge of both the events and the timing of the development and operations of that war. Hence this prologue is an attempt to condense the history of this tremendous undertaking as a background for the events in which my father and I participated.

For those of you who feel no need for this refresher course may I invite you to skip the Prologue and proceed directly to the first chapter.

Pre 1938 – Background for War

By 1936, when this narrative starts, Europe was beginning to heal from the terrible ravages of World War I (1914-1918). "The Great War" had become a bitter and protracted four-year contest that left every one of the participating European Powers totally exhausted, even devastated. The Allies, i.e. France, Great Britain, Italy, Russia, and late in the war the Americans, ultimately prevailed but at the cost of heavy casualties that made destitute both the victors (except the Americans) and the defeated. The Austro-Hungarian Empire, allied with Germany, was effectively eliminated as a nation; after the war she would be divided into the two countries of Austria and Hungary. When Germany finally surrendered in 1918, her Rhineland territory was to be demilitarized permanently and she had to pay heavy reparations to the victors. She lay destitute, plagued with inflation, and emotionally bitter. Alhough the French and British took tremendous losses in manpower, they still retained much of their old colonial empires. Russia saw the Czar deposed and the Leninist revolution install communism as a way of government.

Though Italy had been on the "winning" side in World War I, the nation had emerged in chaos. In 1922 a fascist dictator, Benito Mussolini, had come to power to try to restore order in that nation. He began by rebuilding his army and navy and announced plans to turn the

Mediterranean Sea into "Mare Nostrum" (Our Sea). At first the Italians were delighted that someone had taken charge and made the trains run on time. Though Italy was supposedly a monarchy, Mussolini quickly assumed dictatorial powers.

Germany, under the heavy burden of reparations, could not restart its economy. The result was rampant inflation, hunger, and a complete psychological loss of esteem. Inflation was so bad that there were literally scenes where people wheeled marks (currency) in wheelbarrows to the store, only to find the prices had doubled again and again and they couldn't buy their food. Germany's people were prepared to have anyone take over who could put the country back together and redeem its national honor. Thus the climate was ripe for the creation of the Nazi state and the emergence of Adolph Hitler as its dictator. Hitler immediately found a scapegoat on which to blame Germany's ills – namely the Jews. His first efforts were to force the Jews to relinquish their money and their holdings; later he forced them out of the country. Still later he would introduce the concept of slaughtering the Jews - the "Holocaust".

Hitler immediately began to rearm in earnest. He recognized that only a disciplined nation could recover from the burdens it was carrying. Hence he initiated Youth Groups and other concepts to rebuild a martial spirit among the

Germans. He began to build modern battleships that could meet the British Navy at sea. He invested heavily in dirigibles, such as the *Hindenburg*, as the way of beginning to rebuild an air force and to train pilots. Using the mass psychology of rallies and parades, the Nazi dictator began preparing his people for their eventual return to war.

In Russia things were equally bad. Though the Russian economy was largely agrarian, they too had problems of inflation. Russia had never been a democracy and hence her people, also, were poised for the takeover by a dictator. When the Russian forces were defeated by the German army in World War I, Lenin seized the chance to impose his communist state. The Army and the Navy had revolted and the citizenry rioted in the streets. Later the Czar and his family were murdered. Lenin drove out of the country most of the "monarchists" and laid the rationale for communism in the Soviet Union. Lenin died in 1921 and for three years thereafter there was a power struggle before his later successor, Joseph Stalin, became head of state. Stalin would be the man brutal enough to impose the communist philosophy on the country. By 1936 Stalin had consolidated his power, executed most of the senior officers of his armed forces, and established a very tight dictatorship. He started backing communist movements throughout the world, and re-established his collective economy with a series of five-year plans.

Japan, an island nation like England, had always realized that she had to bring in raw materials if she was to become a world industrial power. Most of the raw materials she needed, such as tin, rubber, iron, coal, and oil, either were imported from the United States or purchased and imported from European colonies such as the Dutch East Indies and French Indo-China. Japan eventually decided to seize what she needed by acquiring possessions in the South Pacific area. This was largely an army strategy; the senior naval officers by and large fought against the idea. However the naval officers did urge the fortification and enlargement of the garrisons of the islands under Japan's influence in the Central Pacific. Thus were developed the great naval bases of Truk and Rabaul.

Once the decision had been made, Japan's first move was to announce the creation of the "Greater East Asian Co-Prosperity Sphere". Then she invaded Manchuria and by 1938 was proceeding down into China. Wracked by a government that was constantly warring with itself, she nonetheless felt that she had to make a move or be completely excluded from being an industrial power.

Great Britain, and to a lesser degree France, had extended their military and economic power far beyond their borders during the preceding centuries. At one point, under Napoleon, France dominated the European continent. Great Britain had a two hundred year history of controlling key defiles of the sea (Gibraltar, Singapore) and her Royal Navy had extended the empire around the world until it could be said that "the sun never sets on the British Empire". However, World War I had taken a heavy toll on their manpower and national treasure, and thus both countries bordered on socialism.

The United States of America, relatively untouched by World War I and still separated by two oceans from the rest of the world, was going through a serious economic recession and a spirit of isolationism. After a riotous time in the 1920's, the country was reeling from the effects of a depressed economy in the 1930's. In 1932 the nation elected Franklin D. Roosevelt as its President and he began his first term by testing various economic and socialist remedies to try to pull the country out of the "great depression".

Although there were, within the meager American armed forces, many visionary men who realized what the change in weaponry that had come about in World War I would mean if we ever went to war again, as a nation we were not ready to accept the cost of building our armed forces. The Naval Treaties between the wars had focused on the relative sizes of naval fleets; sizes of armies were not discussed. General Douglas MacArthur, while Chief of Staff of the Army, had fought Congress for permission to build and experiment with tanks and planes. All this was in vain - in 1936 building an Army and Navy was the lowest priority on Congress' mind.

In summary, by 1938 Japan was attacking China in the Orient; Hitler and Mussolini were dictators of Germany and Italy respectfully and both were building their army, navy and air forces; Russia had become a communist dictatorship under Stalin; France and England were pacifists nations slow to entertain any thoughts about another world war; and the United States was happily isolationist in its own world. This is the background with which this story starts.

1939-1941 – The Axis Apex

The period 1938 through the end of 1941 was the period of great successes by Hitler and his allies (known as the "Axis Powers") during which time Germany conquered much of Europe while Japan reached its outer limit of power in the Pacific. By the end of 1941 Japan had successfully attacked Pearl Harbor and sunk most of our battleships, captured Guam, driven our Philippine Army into Bataan, and conquered much of the East Indies, Singapore, and Malaysia. Germany had conquered and occupied Poland, Norway, the Benelux countries, France, and much of the Libyan/Egyptian Mediterranean Coastline, and vast segments of the Soviet Union.

Great Britain still controlled most of the world's "defiles", the narrow waterways that channel sea borne commerce through them, and thus she continued to rely on this strategy that had made her famous. In the wake of the Spanish Civil War she fortified Gibraltar, which was to remain one of Great Britain's two primary naval bases to control the Mediterranean Sea. She also moved some anti-aircraft guns to the Island of Malta, which sat off Sicily and thus could affect sea traffic through the Med. She reinforced her garrisons in the Far East, primarily with Indian troops, and moved some heavy guns to the fortifications at her naval base at Singapore. She felt she could rely on the loyalty of her various colonies and commonwealths throughout the world, and by and large they did support her. Australian, Canadian, and Indian troops would all play a major part in the battles of World War II. She did bring home most of her Pacific fleet to protect the British Isles.

France was beginning to mobilize but was still depending on its Maginot Line to protect it from invasion from the East. French governments turned over regularly and as a result France had no consistent foreign or economic policy. Many of her officers, such as (then Colonel) Charles DeGaulle, pleaded for the building of mobile forces, but the prevailing military opinion was defensive. The tremendous toll of machine guns in the first war had convinced the French to assume a static defense behind fixed fortifications. The lack of manpower to man these defenses was to be a major contributor to her later defeat by the Germans.

Having analyzed its mistakes in World War I, Germany focused on the concept of a highly mobile striking force led by tanks and supported by dive-bombers. The dive-bomber would replace mobile artillery support. These concepts Hitler tested at length in the Spanish Civil War. Germany was the only power that entered World War II with a predominance of new concepts of warfare based on the new weapons now available. Playing on the theme of "nationalism" and building up German morale, was the most important part of Hitler's agenda at this stage. With the re-occupation of the Rhineland, and the incorporation of Austria into the German camp, the German nation was beginning to feel the return of its pride. They had faced down their WWI enemies successfully. Now they started talking about the "thousand year Reich".

By comparison, in 1938 France and England were totally unprepared for war. Having failed to stand up against Italy when it invaded Ethiopia, and Germany when Hitler made his moves, they now had the job of stopping Hitler from seizing Czechoslovakia. Prime Minister Neville Chamberlain of Great Britain flew to Germany to negotiate peace. These negotiations would convince Hitler that Great Britain did not want to fight under any circumstances. The result of this meeting was the "Munich agreement" in which Hitler alleged no further territorial claims and Chamberlain was able to announce "peace in our time". Only then did Great Britain begin serious rearmament and the building of modern fighter planes such as the Hurricane and the Spitfire.

The United States, also, was totally unprepared for war and in fact still had no plans for serious buildup of its military forces. The major sentiment in the US was isolationism, and we were still trying to pull out of a devastating depression. We were involved in the world scene primarily in the Pacific. Japan needed steel and oil along with other critical raw materials. We began to examine the products we were allowing her to buy from the United States, and would soon put an embargo on selling her steel and scrap iron. Later, in 1941, we would put an embargo on oil and that would trigger Japan's attack on Pearl Harbor.

Finally there were the Balkans. The Balkans were those nations that bordered on, or were south of, the Danube River. That included Albania, Hungary, Romania, Yugoslavia (Slovenia, Croatia, Macedonia, Serbia), Bulgaria, and Greece. Virtually ignored after the end of World War I, both the Axis and the Allied sides would court the Balkan nations. For the British it was a question of making Greece and Crete safe, so as not to allow the Axis to control the Mediterranean. For the Axis powers it was a question of controlling their flank nearest the communist Soviet Union. Russian influence in the Balkans was very strong as they share a Slav culture and the Orthodox Church. The problem with the Balkan states at this time was that all of them appeared to be on the brink of civil war. The arbitrary boundaries drawn up by the victorious Allies after World War I had resulted in the creation of multi-cultural and multi-ethnic states with no central loyalty to a given government nor nationalist spirit to the country as a whole. Loyalties were primarily to local tribes and peoples of the same ethnic and religious background. Sixty years later things have not changed much in this regard.

World War II officially began when, on September 1st 1939, Hitler launched his armies into Poland. Within hours his Luftwaffe had destroyed the Polish air force, and in a blitzkrieg (lightening war) campaign, his new mechanized panzer divisions forced Poland's surrender. In a few weeks the German forces had completely overrun Poland. Two weeks into the campaign Hitler invited Russia to attack from the East under their non-aggression pact. On September 17th, Russian troops moved through the marshes of eastern Poland and closed on the Germans. Hitler then partitioned Poland, giving Stalin the Eastern portion, while Germany took the western section. Thus the German eastern flank was secured and Hitler could use the time before his next campaign, to the west, to mechanize more of his army.

The Soviet Union coupled its late entry into Poland with the quick annexation of the three

Baltic states of Estonia, Latvia and Lithuania. The pact with Hitler had allowed the Soviets to finally get to warm water ports on the Baltic. In November Stalin attacked Finland, expecting an easy take over and the final consolidation of the Soviet's northwest boundaries. What Russian forces thought would be an easy victory turned out to be just the opposite. The Soviets were quickly engaged by the Finns and there ensued a bitter, cold, winter-long fight in which the Finns inflicted heavy losses on the Russian army. Some of Russia's best troops were consumed in this sideline fight. The seizure of these four countries by the Soviets meant that Germany now had a frontier with Russia from the Baltic to the Balkans. This would be very important in Hitler's later plans to invade the Soviet Union.

To Hitler's complete surprise, living up to their treaty obligations to Poland, and finally realizing there was no stopping of Germany short of war, Great Britain and France declared war on Germany on September 3rd, 1939. It was an agonizing decision for British Prime Minister Neville Chamberlain who had hoped to stop Hitler's expansion by diplomacy. By now even the most sympathetic appeasers in Great Britain realized that appeasement would not work. If ever Hitler was to be stopped, the time had come. Thus the British cabinet supported the Prime Minister in declaring war. France was much more reluctant; the French people did not want war. However France was now isolated; her only ally was Great Britain. She had little choice, so she also declared war on Germany.

With the advent of war Chamberlain now brought into his cabinet his long-time political enemy, Winston Churchill. Churchill had spent his years since being the first lord of the Admiralty in World War I trying to wake up Great Britain to the German threat. Now he was vindicated and his services were again needed by his country and so once again he became the First Lord of the Admiralty; what we in America would call the Secretary of the Navy. Thus the stage was set for Churchill to play such a heroic figure in history.

Germany had several large surface ships that she had dispatched to the South and North Atlantic to raid British shipping. One of them, the "pocket battleship" *Graf Spee*, was trapped off Uraguay in South America by three British cruisers and was forced into Montevideo harbor where her crew eventually blew her up. A second raider was the modern German battleship *Bismarck* that went around Scotland with the cruiser *Prince Eugen*. She was spotted by and engaged the brand new *Prince of Wales* and the pride of the British navy, the battlecruiser *HMS Hood.* In three salvos the *Bismarck* hit the *Hood* and caused it to explode, causing the death of all but a few of her crew. Winston Churchill was furious and promptly ordered the bulk of the British fleet out to sea to find and intercept the German vessels. The word was passed to "Sink the *Bismarck*" at all costs. Finally the the British Navy's aircraft carrier *HMS Ark Royal,* flying antiquated Swordfish bi-planes, managed to put a torpedo into *Bismarck's* steering gear thus jamming her rudder and forcing her to go in circles. She continued firing to cover the retreat and escape of the *Prince Eugen*, which successfully returned to Brest in France. The crew of the *Bismarck* took terrible punishment from the big guns of the British battleships that closed in, and the many torpedoes from the British cruisers before she sank. There were few survivors.

Initially Britain's effort was to clear the seas of these raiders, as she feared for the damage they could do to her merchant fleet. However Germany's real strength was in her systematic and well coordinated submarine force. It immediately began to take a heavy toll on allied shipping. England would use its capital ships to contain Hitler's surface navy, but she was desperate for the small destroyers and frigates needed to fight off Germany's U-boats. She adopted the convoy system that had worked so well in World War I.

The British mined much of the North Sea and sent out patrols from Scapa Flow (in north Scotland) but German submarines continued an unrelenting attack on her merchant shipping. One German U-boat commander even managed to slip into the British base of Scapa Flow itself and sink a British battleship at anchor.

The "Battle of the Atlantic", as it was later dubbed, continued unabated until the end of the war. German U-boats roamed the high seas but concentrated on the choke points such as Gibraltar where Allied shipping would congregate to form convoys for the last leg into Great Britain. It would not be until 1943, and the advent of airborne radar and jeep carriers, that the Allies were finally able to turn the tide of this underwater battle.

In early 1940, while the war at sea continued, both Germany and Great Britain saw the strategic importance of Norway and thus both made an attempt to move into Scandinavia. The Germans got there first and conquered Norway, forcing a British withdrawal, and thus insuring Sweden's neutrality and a constant flow of ore to Germany.

Now Hitler was ready for his war of revenge. In the spring of 1940 he launched his attack into France. Positioning his forces in the impenetrable Ardennes Forrest, he massed a heavy assault on one sector of the Maginot Line. At the same time he launched a paratrooper attack on the main bridges in Belgium, and initiated an invasion of Denmark and the Benelux countries. German forces quickly breached the Maginot Line and its Panzer Divisions swept behind the French, English and Belgium forces and drove to the North Sea. Within a few short weeks German forces had trapped the British corps and other Allied forces. The British were forced to evacuate through the small port of Dunkirk, using everything that would float as a rescue vessel including private yachts, fishing boats, etc. It was a remarkable feat but while most of the soldiers got out, most of their equipment had to be left behind. The bulk of the French troops were not rescued and hence were taken prisoner. With this defeat Belgium and the Netherlands surrendered.

The German Panzers then turned from the English channel to sweep through northern France, decimating the French Army as it attacked. The massed tanks in a German Panzer Division would quickly eliminate the French tanks which were distributed among the individual Infantry Divisions. The French Army collapsed and France sued for surrender, agreeing to put the northern half of its country under German occupation, and then forming a puppet government to run the southern half under Field Marshal Petain, an aged French hero from World War I. The Petain government was allowed by the Germans inasmuch as they wished to retain the French fleet – then largely in the ports of Marseille in France and Oran in Morocco. They feared the French would sabotage the fleet, or defect to the British, if they occupied Southern France. (In 1942, when the American forces invaded North Africa, Germany would complete her total occupation of France).

With this defeat Great Britain turned to a new leader. Though he had striven mightily to keep the peace, Neville Chamberlain was now in a war situation and so he stepped down and the British elevated Winston Churchill from First Sea Lord to Prime Minister. At that point England had little or nothing. Although she had salvaged the bulk of her Army Corps in France, but not their materiel, she had few weapons with which to fight other than her Navy which was heavily engaged against the U-boat threat. Great Britain now stood alone in Europe against a triumphant Germany who now was making plans to invade England itself.

Upon taking office as Prime Minister, Churchill announced to Great Britain and the world that he had nothing to offer but "blood, toil, tears and sweat"(1). His oratory and steadfast look, chomping on a cigar as he strode through crisis after crisis, endeared him not only to his own nation but also to the Americans who would gradually become his allies. His bulldog defiant manner would become famous throughout the world.

His first step was to begin reorganizing and re-arming his Army and dispersing the Royal Air Force so that they could not be taken out by one attack. What squadrons he had lent to France now returned to join in the defense of the British Isles. The home guard, made up of volunteers of any age, were trained as militia men. Women joined the armed forces in great numbers, taking on many of the administrative tasks previously done by men, so as to release more men to serve in combat roles. Finally, Churchill began leaning on Roosevelt very heavily in the hopes of bringing America's industrial might, if not America itself, into the conflict on the Allied side.

With the conquest of France complete Germany could now turn its attention to invading Great Britain. While the British frantically tried to rearm and reorganize their troops, the Germans placed their efforts on effecting a channel crossing. They assembled coastal shipping from Calais to Cherbourg, and moved their Luftwaffe in to prepare to soften up the British for an invasion. Field Marshal Hermann Goering, chief of the German Air Force, assured his Fuehrer that he could quickly subdue the Royal Air Force and flatten British cities. Churchill was defiant, and announced in one of his most famous speeches that "... we will fight on the beaches, we shall fight on the landing grounds, we shall fight in the fields and in the streets, we will fight in the hills; we shall never surrender ..." (2)

Hitler commenced his invasion by a prolonged air assault on the British Isles, but in what has become a classic battle of courage the highly outnumbered Royal Air Force stood off the Luftwaffe all fall and won what was to become known as "The Battle of Britain". British Spitfire and Hurricane fighters met the German aircraft as they came over the channel, and is furious dogfights managed to defeat the invaders. Outmaneuvered and outgunned by the British, Marshal Goering then turned to aerial bombing of British cities with the hopes of breaking English morale. Night raids caused extensive fires in London, Manchester, and other industrial centers. The British went underground and remained defiant. Though the bombing did extensive damage to civilian areas, the bombings were very ineffective against the British infrastructure, and it only steeled, not destroyed, British morale. Finally, as a result of his immense aircraft losses, Hitler decided to abandon "Operation Sea Lion" – the invasion of England. In paying tribute to his RAF fighter pilots at a later date Churchill was to say: "Never in the field of human conflict was so much owed by so many to so few."(3)

With the entire European mainland except Portugal, Spain and Switzerland under his domination, Hitler now debated whether to seize the Balkans and the Caucasus or to invade Russia. Hitler needed room for German expansion, his Lebensraum, which was one of his rationales for taking Poland. Both Russia and the Balkans would give him this lebensraum. Though it was unknown to anyone at the time, Hitler decided to invade Russia and began his planning.

By now the United States had begun to realize the facts of Hitler's and the Japanese aggression and thus more and more our sentiment turned to helping the British. Knowing that Great Britain did not have the resources to buy war goods from America, our Congress passed what has come to be known as the "Lend Lease Act", and with it in effect America began in earnest its build up for war. Soon our factories began turning out armaments, planes, and ships that we sent to Great Britain; and we began to rebuild our armed forces through the establishment of the draft system. Our job now was to bring factories on line, reorganize our rail system to provide industrial transportation, obtain and deliver raw materials, and galvanize an army of workers to begin the process of building the weapons of war.

By 1941 Hitler, defeated in the air in 1940's Battle of Britain, had decided to attack the Soviet Union. The German invasion of the Soviet Union changed the course of the war. Until then Germany had been victorious, having overrun most of Europe. However, when the bitter winter closed in on the German forces trying to reach Moscow, Hitler refused to allow his men to retreat to safe lines but instead insisted that they besiege Moscow. It was to be the single biggest mistake Hitler made in the war.

The land battles this year would be tremendous. The German blitzkrieg quickly overran Western Russia, the Ukraine, and the Caucases capturing large segments of the Soviet army. Wherever the army was held up, the Panzers bypassed these areas which the follow-up troops then invested. In the case of Stalingrad the Soviets dug in and fought a protracted battle that would result in the eventual surrender of the German Sixth Army a year later. By and large, however, the Germans were invincible in 1941 and only the bitter winter was able to stop them.

The frigid weather that forced the Germans to hold their positions outside of Moscow gave the Russians time to re-arm and rebuild. While they were under siege, convoys from the United States were beginning to reach Murmask, the USSR's northern port, with planes, tanks and other supplies. These convoys took considerable risk as they had to go around Norway and alongside the Arctic icepack. The perilous journey had to be made in terrible weather, and the convoys were attacked by German U-boats, aircraft and even surface capital ships. The more tonnage that was lost en route the more Stalin cried for additional convoys. In one case, Convoy PQ17, twenty five out of it's thirty seven ships were lost. However, enough got through to save the Russian army.

As the German forces swept through the Soviet Union, Field Marshal Erwin Rommel, probably Germany's greatest tactician, was commanding the German/Italian forces in North Africa. By brilliant maneuvering the "Desert Fox" was able to outflank British positions and destroy large segments of British armor. Italian morale was once again raised as the combined "Africa Corps" drove the superior British forces back to Egypt, where they finally stopped on what became known as the El Alamein line. Rommel could go no further; he had simply run out of supplies. The successful German sweep through the Balkans should have enabled the Germans to send him troops and supplies but the Royal Navy, this time primarily their submarines, sank most of Rommel's support as it crossed the Mediterranean Sea and thus left him exposed and exhausted. Later the British, under British Field Marshal Bernard Montgomery, would counterattack at the battle of El Alamein, and would eventually drive Rommel all the way back to Tunis.

In the Far East Japan continued her conquest of China. However, she began to find it more and more difficult as supplies from the United States began to reach China, and such volunteer groups as the "Flying Tigers" reinforced the Chinese forces. Then, in late July, the United States, Great Britain and the Dutch East Indies decided to impose an oil embargo on Japan. Many people would feel later that Roosevelt did this to invite a Japanese attack. Whatever were his personal motives, the oil embargo certainly triggered a response within the Diet of Japan. She ordered planning for war with the United States.

The idea was not universally popular. Admiral Yamamoto, who had studied in the United States, tried to persuade Prime Minister Konoye of the futility of taking on the great industrial power that America represented. Yamamoto felt he could win the preliminary battles of the first year, but then American industrial capacity would turn the tide against Japan. In October General Tojo replaced Prince Konoye as Prime Minister and he felt that war was necessary if Japan was to survive. Hence Yamamoto was ordered to launch a surprise attack on Pearl Harbor, our major naval base in the Hawaiian Islands. Early in the morning of December 7th, 1941 while Japanese diplomats were negotiating in Washington, his carrier planes devastated Pearl Harbor. That afternoon Japanese aircraft from Formosa attacked Manila and our other air bases in the Philippine Islands, as well as Hong Kong and Malaya. The effects of these attacks were twofold: (1) They were an immediate tactical success and (2) They galvanized the American people and united them under Roosevelt. On December 8th, 1941, the President declared war on Japan; three days later both Hitler and Mussolini, to honor their commitments to Japan, declared war on the United States.

1942-1945 – The Allied Victory

The years 1942-1945 represent the turnaround of the war. For the Allies things were glum at the opening of '42; the British lost Rangoon and Singapore; the Americans lost the Philippines, Wake, and Guam; and the East Indies fell under Japanese domination, The ABCD force lost the battle of the Java Sea, Rommel chased the British back to Egypt, Russian forces were barely holding on, and German U-boats had a stranglehold on the British Isles.

But then, as the impact of our tremendous industrial power began to be felt in refurbishing armies, navies and air fleets throughout the world, things began to change. In the Pacific, the spring of 1942 saw the great aircraft carrier battles of the Coral Sea and Midway, where Admiral Nimitz broke the back of the Japanese naval air strength. One of the key factors in the Battle of Midway had been the successful breaking of the Japanese Naval Code by the United States. The Japanese opened the battle by bombing Midway and preparing to send in a landing force, while their carrier planes searched in vain for our ships. We in turn first launched our torpedo bombers against their carriers but all of our planes were shot down, doing minimal damage. Later, however, our dive bombers found the Japanese and very quickly sank all four of their carriers.. In one brief battle, American naval pilots had decimated the Japanese carrier fleet.

In the summer of 1942, on Guadalcanal, first Marines and then Army troops successfully held on to the strategic Solomon Islands even though it cost us heavily in lost ships. Our planes from Henderson Field (Guadacanal) managed to attack and shoot down Admiral Yamamoto's plane, killing him. General MacArthur's Australian troops successfully defended Port Moresby, stopping any further expansion of the Japanese to the south; then he began his island hopping campaign up New Guinea to recapture the Philippines.

In North Africa in August, the British Eighth Army finally defeated the German Africa Corps at the battle of El Alamein outside of Egypt. They then began the long task of pushing Rommel's forces back across North Africa, driving him finally into Tunisia. In November the Americans would conduct their first European offensive by landing at Oran and Casablanca, and driving east. After several local defeats, the American and British forces joined up at Tunis and forced the surrender of what was left of the Africa Corps.

From England the British began the heavy strategic bombardment campaign against Germany and occupied France. The British bombed mainly at night. Later they were joined by American units in what became, in time, the US Eighth Airforce. Flying B-17s and 24s, the Americans began daylight strategic bombing missions first against industrial targets, then in support of our ground troops, and finally on German cities. To this day the results of the heavy bomber campaign are still debated; certainly the cost was very high in lost British and American crews.

Now American production began to kick in in earnest. In New Orleans a gentleman by the name of Higgins started building landing craft. Our aircraft factories began to turn out modern fighter planes such as the P-38, F6U, P-47 and the P-51, and the hundreds of B-17s and B-24 bombers that we would need to conduct the war. Along with airplanes, all the other materials for war – guns, food, medicines, vehicles, etc – were coming off the assembly line in droves. America went on a rationing program for meat, tires, and gasoline. Civilians collected aluminum pots and pans and turned them in to be re-fabricated into aircraft. As our draft called up large bodies of men, women took over the running of machines. Posters of "Rosie the Riveter" began showing up on walls, as did a picture of Uncle Sam urging everyone to buy war bonds.

Finally, on the West Coast, Henry Kaiser began to build cargo ships, dubbed "Liberty" or "Victory", and tankers, by prefabrication at a pace that no one had foreseen. At last replacement ships were being built faster than the German U-boats could sink them. It was a phenomenal feat. It was these ships that successfully transported the fighting materials to the British, Russians, and Chinese in giant convoys, and would later permit the deployment of United States forces throughout the world.

In addition to gearing up our industrial might, we had the very practical job of building an Army, Navy and Air Force almost from scratch.

Training fields for pilots began to dot the landscape. Old Army posts were refurbished with new barracks, chapels, mess halls, and training facilities. New posts and naval bases were acquired and built up. It was a monumental effort and while the credit for its success goes to millions of people, the credit for the leadership of this effort goes primarily to General George Marshall, the Army's Chief of Staff. Marshall appointed one of the more famous early pilots, General "Hap" Arnold, to take over the building of the air armada.

In 1943, Allied Forces finally assumed the offensive around the world. In the Mediterranean United States and British troops launched a combined airborne and sea assault on Sicily and secured it. They then continued on to land in Italy. Under terrible fighting conditions our forces worked their way up the Italian Peninsula with heavy fighting between Salerno and Rome. On July 25th Mussolini was forced to resign, and on September 3rd Italy surrendered and switched to the Allied side. It was hoped that this attack in Italy would tie up a large portion of the German army and require that they take troops away from the Russian front to fight here, but the German defense was so effective and the mountainous territory so difficult that the Italian campaign failed in this regard, and it became a long slow, slugging match until the end of the war.

With the coming of radar, jeep carriers (merchant ships with a flight deck and a small detachment of aircraft), and increased destroyers, we began to break the back of the German U-boat offensive. German submarine losses became huge and their ability to supply their vessels with fuel oil through cargo type submarines was not effective. The result of our successful counteroffensive against the U-boat was a great increase in supplies to the Soviet Union and the United Kingdom. A refurbished Russian army began to drive the Germans back. In the meanwhile great quantities of supplies were delivered to England for the eventual invasion of the Continent.

In February the battle for Stalingrad was over; the Russians had finally forced the surrender of Germany's Sixth army. The USSR began going on the offensive and engaged the German armored forces in the great tank battles around Kursk and Rostov. In bitter fighting and taking tremendous casualties, both military and civilian, the Russians in 1943 and 1944 would effect the collapse of the entire German effort in the Soviet Union, and then the huge Russian forces would drive through Poland and on to Berlin.

In the mid-Pacific the Marines made a series of landing through the Gilbert and Marianas island chains that would culminate in the capture of Iwo Jima and Okinawa. The Japanese fought desperately with very few of their troops surrendering. Further, as we neared their home islands in attacking Iwo Jima and Okinawa the fanaticism of the Japanese reached its zenith with the decision to send their planes to crash into American ships. These kamikaze reaped a heavy toll on the supporting naval fleets.

With the capture of Iwo and Okinawa, American long range bombers could now start pounding Japan itself, burning out most of the cities of Japan. Using an even longer range bomber than previously, the B-29, we were able to hit most of the Japanese industrial base, and military and naval installations. Later these planes would be joined by carrier borne planes from the US fleet which would cause "firestorms" in the cities they raided, quickly burning up the bamboo and paper houses for which Japan is famous.

General MacArthur's forces fought their way up New Guinea and finally landed at Leyte in the Philippine Islands, thus making good on his pledge in 1942 that "I shall return". This was crucial to Japan, as they recognized that the recapture of the Philippines would mean the end of their supply line from the Dutch East Indies. Our forces in the Philippines would sit astride this main supply route and it would be quickly cut off. Thus the Japanese were forced to react, which they did in deciding to commit the remainder of their Navy in one last all-out effort. This multi-faced battle, which saw everything from cruisers being attacked by PT boats, small carriers being shelled by battleships, and finally the last great battleship-to-battleship naval gun battle, has gone down in history as the Second Battle of the Philippine Sea. By the end of the fight the Japanese navy had been eliminated as an effective fighting force, and the American navy now ruled supreme in the Pacific. Planes from its aircraft carriers could join the B-29s flying from Iwo Jima to rain destruction upon Japan itself.

Even before this battle, US submarines had gradually cut the strategic supply lines between Japan and the East Indies. Operating out of Pearl Harbor and Australia our submarines took a heavy toll not only on Japanese commercial shipping but also of their warships. They also picked up many a pilot who had been downed by Japanese fire. The submarine siege of the islands of Japan proved the effectiveness of commerce raiding as a weapon of war. By the end of the war our submarines had penetrated the Sea of Japan itself, and were sinking small coastal shipping between Japan and the Korean Peninsula.

On June 6th, 1944 Allied Armies in Italy had forced the surrender of Rome. However this feat was overshadowed by what became to be known as "D-Day"; the day of the Allied attack from Great Britain over the beaches of Normandy. In what would go down as the greatest amphibious landing in history, Allied Forces managed to put ashore over 100000 men on the first day despite a desperate fight on "Omaha" beach. Led by the dropping of three airborne divisions behind the lines in the early morning hours and then a heavy bombardment of the beach defenses by both aircraft and line naval units, the landing in Normandy was a singular achievement in warfare. Eisenhower had gambled on a one-day break in the weather to force a stormy but successful crossing of the English Channel. This was followed by a tremendous over-the-beach logistical operational and the buildup of four armies on the shore. The airborne assault had scattered paratroopers over a large section of Normandy, and most of these units failed to achieve their objectives. However, the German command was greatly confused by the reports of parachute landings in so many different places, and thus the airborne assault materially aided the later over-the-beach landings.

Once ashore, the Allied armies tried to break out and capture the port of Cherbourg. However, difficult hedgerow fighting slowed down the Allied attack. Finally, after two months, a breakout was achieved at St. Lo. Immediately the US Third Army under General George Patton led the drive across France and into Germany. Swinging around the German forces from the south, Patton joined with the British forces from Caen, thus trapping the bulk of the German forces in France in what has come to be known as the Falaise Pocket. Then the armies drove on toward the Rhine, hampered only by the inability of the supply forces to keep up. The logistics people opened what was called the "Red Ball" express, where army trucks would haul supplies coming over the beach long distances to the rear of the fighting armies, and then return by a different route for another load. It was a phenomenal logistics feat; however we still were not able to get enough fuel up to Patton's armored forces to allow him to maintain his momentum. Later we would also run short of artillery shells.

As the drive continued it appeared that the German army had been completely disrupted. We found out that Field Marshal Rommel, now commanding the German forces in France, had been hurt in an automobile strafing, and it appeared that the German effort in the West would collapse. As our forces neared the Rhine the German resistance grew stronger, and the fighting much harder. Nonetheless it appeared by late fall that Germany would be defeated in 1944.

It was not to be. Just before Christmas of 1944, the Germans staged a well-prepared and well planned counterattack against the Allied Forces in what has become to be known as the "Battle of the Bulge". It temporarily disrupted the Allied offensive and threw its forces on the defensive as they tried to protect the port of Antwerp. Only hard fighting on the Allied side, overwhelming air superiority, plus the spirit of the 101st Airborne Division that refused German ultimatums to surrender, managed to stop the Germans. For many days inclement weather gave the German Panzers cover from our air support; but when the weather cleared General Patton was able to drive his forces to relieve the siege of Bastogne. Once that was accomplished the steam came out of the German attack and gradually we recovered the lost territory and pushed the German army back across the Rhine river.

In September of '44, in the northern sector, British Field Marshal Bernard Montgomery had attempted a costly airborne attack into the Netherlands. Although the initial parachute drop of the Allied First Airborne Army was a success, the follow-up land forces were unable to reach the foremost units and thus the battle was a failure. However, Montgomery was now securely in Holland and approaching German soil from the north. Now he launched his final offensive that would see him recapture Holland, Belgium and Denmark. He also was able to eliminate the German's V-1 and V-2 offensive that was hurting London. The V-1s and V-2s were unmanned rockets fired from the northern coast of Europe across the channel. The V-1 was essentially a small airplane, rocket powered, which could be detected and shot down by British fighter aircraft. The V-2 however, was the forerunner of today's rocketry. It traveled at speeds far in excess of anything that the world knew up to that time. There was no defense against them as they could not be detected. Only eliminating their launch pads could stop the V-2 bombardment of London. After the war, modifications of the V-2 would one day serve as launching vehicles for our astronauts into space.

In the center sector, US General Omar Bradley had finally penetrated Germany before the Germans counterattacked in their Ardennes offensive. Once "the Bulge" had been eliminated and his First US Army was reorganized, it began to race to the Rhine. There, with great luck, they captured the big railroad bridge at Remagen intact. Courageously charging across it, they were able to roll many troops over it before the bridge collapsed. Fortunately, by that time, they had been able to put pontoon bridges in place and continue their thrust East into Germany. Only in the complex of the Saar and Moselle Rivers, known as the "Siegfried Switch", were the Germans able to hold up the US Third Army. Clearing out this triangle was imperative. Once the Allies did that all the armies could converge on the Ruhr, the great industrial base of the Germans, and then continue east to meet the Russians on the Elbe River.

On the Russian front the Soviet Union first recaptured Warsaw and then all of Poland. Her forces seized the Balkans and Austria as she closed in on Germany. By April she had surrounded and besieged the German capital of Berlin. In bitter hand to hand fighting she gradually took the city which finally surrendered on May 2nd. With it she captured the Reichstag building in which were the bunkers where Hitler was hiding. While there is no ultimate proof that they recovered his body, it is firmly believed that Hitler took his own life and that of his mistress, Eva Braun, and that their bodies were doused with gasoline and cremated.

As the British and Americans drove east across Germany they finally met the Russians along the Elbe River. With conquest complete, they accepted Germany's surrender on May 7, 1945; thereafter known as "V-E" day. The joint forces celebrated each other and their victory.

In the Pacific, American forces retook the Philippine Islands and prepared for the invasion of Japan itself. General MacArthur drew up plans for a direct assault on Japan's home islands. It would be costly in casualties for the Japanese were fanatical in their defenses despite the fact that our bombing campaign had reduced most of Japan to rubble. MacArthur had bypassed over two million Japanese troops in his island hopping campaign, but there were still plenty of soldiers on Japan proper to make our invasion very expensive in manpower losses. Concurrently Lord Mountbatten's Allied (mainly British) forces began driving back the Japanese in China, Burma and India.

Then, in August, President Truman ordered the use of the atomic bombs that we had been secretly building since the outset of the war. The first was dropped on the Japanese city of Hiroshima on August 6th. Despite the surprise and devastation that this invoked, and the chaos in the Diet and war cabinet, the Japanese elected to continue to fight. Then on August 9th the United States dropped the second atomic bomb on Nagasaki. That did it. Disregarding any objections his war cabinet might have advanced, the Emperor personally ordered his nation to surrender. From then on not a shot was fired by the Japanese, though many of their officers committed harikari. The surrender was accepted by General MacArthur on board the battleship

Missouri on September 2, 1945 - "VJ Day". The greatest war in history was over!

Immediately, US troops began occupying the main Japanese islands, while other allied troops reoccupied the Dutch East Indies, Singapore, and all the other territories that had been seized by the Japanese. Units of the Japanese fleet surrendered or were scuttled. General MacArthur was made the Supreme Military Commander over Japan; a position which he executed with such finesse and expertise that he would become a hero to the Japanese nation upon his departure six years later.

World War II thus ended in the complete victory of the Allied Forces. The United States, "the Arsenal of Democracy", emerged as the most powerful nation in the world. The years following the war saw us bringing home our troops, and many of our dead. But the majority of our casualties lie in American cemeteries throughout the world ... the many *fields of crosses* created for the final resting place of our honored dead.

PHOTOGRAPHS

1. Top: Captain Louis J. Fortier, US Army
2. Bottom: Solidelle Renshaw, soon to become Mrs. Fortier
3. Top: Captain Fortier with his newly born son, Fort Stotsenburg, Philippine Islands, 1924.
4. Bottom Left: Author at Fort Sill, OK 1927
5. Bottom Right: Mother and Dad in New Orleans, LA shortly after their marriage in the fall of 1918
6. Top: The three children of Solidelle and Louis Fortier on or about 1930. (left to right) : author, Margot and Solidelle
7. Bottom left: Author at Fort Hoyle, 1935
8. Bottom right: Mother with my sister Margot, Fort Leavenworth, KS, circa 1932
9. Top Right: Mother, Father, Author and Younger sister Margot sitting in a park in Paris, 1937
10. Top Left: Margot and the author in the French Alps, 1937
11. Center: Our cook buying a chicken to bring home, Belgrade, Yugoslavia in 1939
12. Bottom Left: Our houseman, housemaid and cook in Belgrade, 1939
13. Bottom Right: Typical scene in Belgrade in 1940 – horses were still the principal means of transportation.

CHAPTER ONE

Pre 1937: Father

My paternal grandfather, Joseph Edgar Fortier, was born and raised on one of the old plantations along the Mississippi that still existed after the Civil War. He was a graduate of Jefferson college, the premier Louisiana college of its time. For a while he operated the plantation, but then was tempted to get involved in Honduras in a gold mining venture. It wiped him out and he returned a broken man. He settled in Gretna, Louisiana, a small town just outside of New Orleans, where he ran a grocery store until, like so many other small retailers of the depression, he was again wiped out when the people to whom he extended credit could not repay him. He died in 1927 leaving behind him three sons and two daughters, and a wonderful widow, my grandmother, who would live to the age of one hundred and one.

Louis Joseph Fortier, born in 1892 in the town of Gueydan, Louisiana, was the eldest son (though an earlier child had been lost at six months of age). He attended Chenet Institute, a private school for boys, and at the age of sixteen received an honorary scholarship to Tulane University in New Orleans. During this period of his life his mother was his inspiration and model. She had been born in 1865, the last year of the "War Between the States", and she told wonderful stories about plantation life in the sixties and seventies, about Yankee carpetbaggers, and about "Beast Butler", the Union General who had occupied New Orleans during the late war. Like most people of New Orleans of French linage, she spoke fluent French and hence my father became bi-lingual at an early age. Because of her ancestral heritage Dad would become a member of the Sons of the American Revolution, the War of 1812 Society, the Veterans of the Mexican War, and, of course, the Sons of the Confederacy. Because of the poverty of his father, Dad was to contribute to her support for the rest of his life.

In 1913 he became a distinguished engineering graduate from Tulane. During the summers, and after he graduated, my father worked for the Corps of Engineers surveying what was to become the Intercostal Waterway in southern Louisiana. This gave him practical engineering experience and the joy of being out in a small boat in the Louisiana bayous. There, Dad developed his love for duck hunting and fishing. He would tell us tales of shooting mallards in such quantity that they would fill the small pirouts (canoe-like boats propelled by pushing poles through the bayous) almost to the point of sinking. Game was abundant. The bayous contained all

49

forms of wild life including snakes, the one thing of which he was afraid. Fish abounded and many a day, when he wasn't running a transit, he would put a line over the side and catch fish. He never lost his love for his hunting and fishing and my last photo of my father was on a freezing day in a duck blind in Currituck, NC. He was then in his late seventies.

In addition to his love for hunting and fishing, he loved a good poker or bridge game. After he retired from the military service he spent much of his time at the Army Navy Club in Washington, DC playing cards with his old friends. They tell me he was a highly analytical competitor with a phenomenal memory for what card had been played or how the bidding had gone. He told me he had learned to play cards while on those surveying missions out in the bayous. He was a true Creole. He loved his bourbon, his thick New Orleans black coffee, his gumbo and jambalaya. Later in World War II, after he had been selected to be a general, he picked an aide-de-camp. According to that aide, who turned out to be Gary Black, the son of the publisher of the "Baltimore Sun", my father's criteria for selecting his aide was the latter's ability to make, and drink, the thick black coffee he so loved. Gary felt all other criteria were secondary. They became close friends as well as comrades-in-arms.

In many ways he appeared to be a very complex man in that he often appeared to be a "loner" yet he had a wide list of friends and acquaintances. His friends described him as a happy man who seemed to be able to roll with life's punches and was in continuing good humor. He was also noted, however, for his complete honesty. A man of towering intellect and a tremendous student of both history and geography, he was a strategic thinker and had a "feel" for world events in historical perspective. These traits alone would make him a great intelligence officer but he was also gifted with one other trait – the ability to consume considerable alcohol without ill effect. I often suspected he was simply clever at pouring his drink into the nearest potted plant, but however he did it he was destined to glean a huge amount of "intelligence" upon which his reputation would rest.

When World War I broke out, Dad entered the Army reserves but was immediately commissioned a second lieutenant. During the war he was dispatched overseas where he served most of his battlefield tour with the French Army as a liaison officer from the US 2nd Infantry Division. Though a bullet or piece of shrapnel passed through his riding trousers while he was delivering a message during that conflict, he returned unscathed a year later and decided to make the Regular Army his career. He told me that the experiences of his father, plus his need to support his mother, played a large role in his selecting a steady career with guaranteed retirement.

Before the war his best friend, Donald Renshaw, had introduced Dad to his younger sister, Solidelle. She was a lovely young lady from a prominent New Orleans family. She was one of the youngest of thirteen children. Her father had fought in the battle of Shiloh and thus she was to later become a "real daughter" in the "United Daughters of the Confederacy". As soon as Dad returned home from France, and after a short courtship her father, Judge Henry Renshaw, gave his consent to the nuptials. They married in September of 1918. She bore him two daughters, Solidelle Felicite and Margot Helene, and one son. I am privileged to be that son.

From 1918 Dad, like so many officers of his era, spent the next seventeen years as a captain of Field Artillery. In those days duty for Army officers seemed to be a continuing routine change from schooling to troop command. Thus, after his first troop assignment, he enjoyed a tour at Auburn University in Alabama where he served as the Ass't PMS&T (Professor of Military Science and

Tactics). He loved being back in the South, and it was at Auburn, in 1921, that his first child, my older sister Solidelle, was born. She obviously inherited Dad's analytical skills as she became a genius at solving puzzles of any kind – cryptogram, crossword, you name it – and later received her doctorate in economics and delivered many papers both in the United States and abroad. While at Auburn Dad received his Masters Degree (summa cum laude) in International Relations, after which he was sent back to troop duty – this time to the Philippine Islands.

The only story he ever related to me about Luzon was the excitement in his command, the 24th Field Artillery Philippine Scouts, when they took part in the suppression of the Moro uprising in the Philippine Islands in the 1920s. One of the sergeants in his battery had gone out on patrol ... and failed to return. Several days later a pack mule came back to the post with saddlebags over its back. When the bags were opened they found the sergeant chopped into small chunks by a machete. This gave a real impetus to the hunt, but I understand his outfit never found the group that committed the crime.

Needless to say, in this author's opinion, the biggest event of the Philippine tour was the birth of his only son.

Upon his return from the Philippines he was assigned command of an artillery battery at Fort Sill, Okla. Fort Sill was (and is today) the Army's training ground for artillerymen. His job was to take fledgling artillery officers out on the range and teach them how to control the fire of cannons. It was hot and dusty work, but he loved it. While there he also had the opportunity to study the campaigns of the Army against the Plains Indians, whom he greatly admired for their mobility. He used to compare them to Russia's Cossacks as first class cavalrymen. While he commanded troops at Fort Sill, Dad tied for the coveted "Knox Trophy" award for the best battery in the army. He apparently was a very devoted but down-to-earth officer to whom the troops could relate. The fact that he was upbeat most of the time, and not too strict on army discipline, made him a good battery commander.

His favorite story about his duty at Fort Sill was in connection with his experience as a lawyer. In those days when a soldier did something wrong and was court-martialed, he was allowed to pick any officer to defend him. One of the soldiers of

54

his battery was caught red handed stealing gasoline in the middle of the night from the Post gas station. The MPs stopped him just as he was driving off and he confessed to them. As far as my father could see the case was an open and shut proposition; there was no defense. Then it occurred to Dad to check at the gas station the records of the clerk who had closed the station that night, and who had logged what each pump read. Knowing how lazy clerks can be Dad checked the records of the clerk that opened the station the next day. Just as suspected, the morning clerk had not gone out to check the pumps, he simply entered the closing figures of the day before. Result – there was no crime (no gas was recorded as missing) and therefore no criminal. When the boy was acquitted Dad became very popular as the defense counsel of choice as long as he remained at Fort Sill.

The true importance of Fort Sill was the birth of my younger sister Margot. My Mother and Father has been married for three years when my older sister was born, I was born three years after that, and now the next three year cycle saw the birth of the last of the children. Margot was to become my close companion and loving pal through all the period related in this chronology, and remains so today. Like myself, she would have five children but she far outnumbers both myself and my older sister in the grandchild division, having a dozen of them. She would marry a naval officer who had five sea commands during his twenty eight years of distinguished service; needless to say he was loved by his father-in-law who could fully appreciate his career. Margot inherited many of my father's Creole traits, including his love of crabs and gumbo, and, like her sister, his analytical skills. I have never been able to beat her in a game such as Scrabble or at doing crossword puzzles. After Dad died Margot took over the care of our Mother and nursed her through her difficult declining years. I have always loved her and she is still my sweetheart today.

Dad spent several years in Oklahoma before he received a two-year tour at Fort Leavenworth, Kansas. Fort Leavenworth was (and is) the home of the Army's Command and General Staff School and thus was the next step in the alternate pattern of school/command/school/command that was the life of the regular service officer. Selection to attend C&GS was considered a necessity if one was ever to become a general officer. This was the army's school for studying the integration of the respective army arms such as artillery, infantry, engineers, chemical warfare, quartermaster, etc. After schooling at Leavenworth it was back to troops; we proceeded to Pennsylvania where Dad was given responsibilities with the Pennsylvania National Guard. Living in Radnor, just outside of

Philadelphia, Dad toured the State training Guard troops. The National Guard at that time had more troops than did the Regular Army, and the Guard would play a critical role when the Army mobilized for World War II. Some of the heaviest casualties during the war would be taken by Guard divisions.

While there, Dad was assigned to open and run a "CCC Camp". The Civilian Conservation Corps was one of the things that President Roosevelt had created to fight the depression. The men would volunteer for this semi-military organization to do civilian projects such as building roads, cutting timber, and constructing dams, etc. Although he had military jurisdiction over these people, he and his fellow military officers realized that they could not simply order these people around; they had to be led, coached, trained and supervised without the backing of military order. As it got colder and colder in the CCC camp in Ridgeway, Pennsylvania, many of the men simply left. Dad would tell me later that he never understood how George Washington was able to keep so many of his troops in camp during the bitter winter in Valley Forge, PA.

Having served with troops the next cycle was schooling once again; so he spent 1935-36 at the Army War College in Washington, D.C. Once again his love for study and analysis was to pay off. At the War College Dad did a detailed study of the "Battle of the Crater" of the Civil War, which was so well done that it was introduced into the curriculum and used for later classes. His interests, however, were not in doing the study but, being an engineer by training, he was interested in how effective fortifications were and how difficult they were to breach. The "Battle of the Crater" in Petersburg was just such an instance.

In 1864, as the Union Army encircled both Richmond and Petersburg, Grant found it impossible to effect a break through the Confederate lines. Individual assaults had been repulsed with heavy casualties. Then his Pennsylvanian miners conceived the idea of digging under Lee's line of fortifications and planting underground explosives to blow a hole in the Confederate defenses, thus allowing Union troops to pour through. The tremendous explosion, that created the crater that can still be seen today, ripped open Lee's lines as planned. However the Union forces failed to capitalize on the breech and Lee was able to plug the hole in time. Dad felt that if Grant had rushed up cavalry instead of infantry he could have carried the day. Dad was not to forget this lesson when he later studied the French Army's static defense line and the German "blitzkrieg" tactics. He became convinced that with mobile forces Germany could exploit a breach through the Maginot Line if they could effectively punch a hole through it … exactly what the Germans did in 1940 in the Ardennes Forest when they later invaded France.

Back in those days there was an old Army custom. Protocol required that each officer assigned to duty in Washington, and his wife, make a courtesy call on the Commander-in-Chief (The President). Apparently this was a tradition started back in Thomas Jefferson's term of office. Mother used to tell of her "mortifying" experience when the time came for them to make their call. It was understood that one only called on a day that the President and his wife would not be at home; that way one could leave his card and get credit for doing his duty. So one day, when he got the word that the President was on the road, Mother, in mid-day clothes, and Dad called on the White House. They dropped their cards and were in the act of departing when Mrs. Roosevelt walked in. Mother was mortified, felt totally undressed, and thought she had ruined Dad's career. It turned out that Mrs. Roosevelt was most entertaining for about a half hour before they departed. Nonetheless Mother never liked Eleanor Roosevelt after that.

Upon graduation from the War College Dad returned to troop duty; this time at Fort Hoyle, MD, with the 1st Field Artillery Brigade.. His unit was given the job of evaluating the new ordnance, namely 105mm howitzers, being developed at the nearby Aberdeen Proving Ground. They would take them out on the range in all kinds of weather to see how well they could "take it" when under battlefield conditions. During this tour he was finally promoted, in 1935, to major. This promotion made him the Operations Officer of the battalion, and thus the analysis and follow-up reports on the howitzers fell to him. Dad was never a mechanically oriented individual but rather a strategic thinker. He found this duty to be very technical and therefore very boring. Nonetheless he had a happy family at Fort Hoyle on the scenic Chesapeake Bay, and thus he still enjoyed that short tour of duty.

It was to be a short tour for, in 1937, the idyllic life on the Chesapeake was cut short. He received orders to go to Paris to attend the vaunted French War College – "L'Ecole Superieur de Guerre". Both Mother and Dad were thrilled with this assignment. Mother would enjoy the travel; Dad would enjoy meeting foreign officers with new ideas and strategies. It did not take long to pack up the household goods and to report to New York to take the trip over.

Taking his family with him, he spent two years in France studying the tactics and grand strategy of World War I. He thoroughly enjoyed the camaraderie of the French officers (remember he was bilingual) as well as getting to know the foreign officers, particularly the Germans, who were at the school. He told me later how diligently the German officers studied the German attack in World War I, analyzing and reanalyzing it to determine why the Allies were able to stop them at the Marne. They also tried to study the Maginot Line as best they could, but the French were not showing off most of it to the foreign officers, particularly the Germans. Because he was bilingual and considered "one of them" by the French officers, Dad was fortunate to be allowed to visit a much larger portion of the line than his fellow foreign officers. There were over fifty foreign officers in his class, officers from armies all over the world. The French instructors, naturally, tended to present combat from the French point of view. However the analyses and discussions with all these foreign officers was, for Dad, the real learning experience. He realized then how many new ideas and how much creative thinking was going on throughout the world as new weapons and concepts in using them developed. He told me later he tried to put out of his mind all that he had learned at the American schools of war (the Command and General Staff school and the Army War College) and to listen to his classmates' imaginative thinking. It was going to turn out for him to be an experience he truly enjoyed.

The German officers particularly fascinated him. They loved to ask questions about mobile war, tanks, fuel supplies, and air support. The Italians had been one of the early prophets of massed air power; a concept of strategic bombing that Great Britain and the US would later adopt. The Germans, however, felt that aircraft should be used to give the troops on the ground tactical mobility and firepower support. These conflicting concepts in aerial warfare would be debated at great length in the American army that was finally created for World War II. We would end up creating two separate air forces, one tactical for ground support, one strategic for long range bombing.

Another study that fascinated Dad was the analysis of logistics. France relied heavily on their excellent rail system to move supplies and troops forward and laterally. The Germans were building superior highways, the Autobahn system, which would enable them to shuttle mechanized forces around quickly, and relieve their dependence on rail lines that could be destroyed from the air by bombs. (In America at this time we had no such concept as the autobahn, in fact it would be brought back from Germany to us after the war by President Eisenhower who created our Interstate road system of today.) The autobahn system enabled Germany, even at the height of the war, to move the products of their factories to their troops in the field. After they had occupied France, the Germans had to depend on the French rail system for logistics. Thus our bombers from England, and French saboteurs, were able to disrupt much of their logistical and tactical movements; validating the Germans' original ideas about the autobahns.

Being an artilleryman Dad was most interested in what the other nations were doing in this field. He was disappointed to find that the French were still using their World War I vintage "seventy fives". He was surprised to learn that the Germans also had not really progressed in artillery. However, the difference was that the Germans had given up the idea of artillery support in favor of tactical aircraft. They had developed the Junkers 88 and Stuka dive bombers to the point that they could cover their infantry and armor on the ground from the air, thus alleviating the need to haul cannons around the battlefield. However, they never learned to use concentrated artillery the way the Americans did, and that provided us with a distinct advantage when we finally got into the war.

While representing the United States at the French War College, my father also had orders to send back to the War Department any information he might develop on the French or other European armies. With his class having so many foreign officers from armies around the world he could be a good source of intelligence for America. While we had a Military Attache at the American Embassy in Paris, my father as a student had more opportunity to see French installations and talk with French officers than did the Embassy people. And so he took these orders seriously and faithfully reported everything he could about the strength and composition of the French and other armies. . As he found out later this was not always appreciated at home ... and it was to get him into trouble soon.

Pre 1937: Son

While serving in the Philippines, Captain Fortier saw the birth of his only son in 1924. Needless to say the son does not remember the Philippines of those days though he did get a chance to see Manila in 1945. By then his birthplace, the old Fort Stotsenburg, had become Clark Field and his birthplace no longer existed. Devastated by the terrible hand-to-hand fighting that had just taken place a few months before, the city of Manila lay in ruins and its harbor was a forest of masts of sunken ships.

My young life was spent on Army posts in the mid-west. My earliest recollections are of Fort Sill, Oklahoma. I still remember the cannon booming when they lowered the garrison's flag at five every afternoon, and the haunting music of both "tattoo" and "taps" which were blown by a bugler at, I believe, ten at night. I recall the clatter and clanging of the caissons and cannons being drawn by horses going out to the field every day, and the rattle of firing which would drift in from the rifle and pistol firing ranges in the afternoons. It was hot and dusty at places like Fort Sill and the cannoneers with their horses and caissons, could truly sing the Artillery song: "Over hill, over dale we have hit the dusty trail".

The rest of my recollections of my early years are vague. I believe what both my sisters and I remember best are the long automobile trips taken on semi-paved or dirt roads as we drove from one army post to another in the mid-west.

We drove long hours, there was no such thing as air-conditioning, and rest stops were few and far between. We played all the usual automobile games such as identifying the license plates of the various states, but I think we spent the bulk of our time fighting with one another in the back seat, or begging our parents to stop so we could go to the bathroom. Then I remember that when we did stop, and I was ready to burst, Mother had to first scour the bathroom with Lysol. The additional delay was agonizing, and the fact that the girls got to go first did little to enhance my ideas of chivalry.

Today with our Interstate highways and frequent "rest areas" for gasoline and food stops, most of us have a hard time remembering our pre-WWII road net. While many roads were paved, many were not, and three or four lane roads were almost non-existent. Traveling through the dust bowl of the thirties in the Oklahoma area I can vividly recall clouds of windblown sand and dirt blowing into the windows that we had to keep open because of the heat. I remember when we would unpack at night our possessions would be covered in grit and dust. Many times river crossings were fords, and one crossed a stream by fording a depression in the riverbank rather than crossing a bridge. I can still remember my first automobile accident when a farmer's old truck, far

66

overloaded with produce, crossed a ford in front of us and started up the other embankment, only to have the engine fail and to roll backwards towards us. Fortunately, Dad was able to swerve and avoid the truck hitting us, but we did have to get out and give the farmer a hand to get his truck pulled out of the river, reloaded and restarted.

We were at Fort Leavenworth in Kansas at the height of the depression. Because Dad worked for the Government on a regular income we were not materially affected by it, but we did see lots of starving families on the road. I remember that Mother always had some extra food on hand and when one of these men would knock on the door and ask for work, she always found some sort of job for them and then would feed them a good meal and give them some money before sending them on their way. She tried to explain to us who these people were and why they were forced to drift. She even tried to get us to put aside a little bit of our allowances to give to the poor. I don't remember her being too successful at teaching us the giving of alms. I can remember being sassy one day when I was asked to do some chore and I suggested to Mother that she wait until one of the drifters came by; that they would tackle it. I believe I spent the rest of that day in my room.

Today, as we live in a land of abundance and wealth, while there is still serious poverty particularly in some of the urban areas, most of us really do not realize how devastating poverty can be on a man's morale and honor. These drifters were good people who were just down on their luck. The combination of a long draught in the Midwest, and the 1930 era depression, reduced many a good man to hopelessness and drifting. It helps to remember this as we see World War II developing and we wonder why so many states were turning to fascism or dictatorships in their desperation.

As we drove from Kansas, where he had attended the Command and General Staff School, Dad tried to explain to us the Oklahoma and Southwest Indian cultures and territories. But at ten years of age I was not very interested in Plains Indians. What I was interested in were the Iroquois; I loved reading the "Leatherstocking Tales" by James Fenimore Cooper. I could just see myself stalking through thick virgin forests avoiding Indian trails. Thus Dad's later assignment to Fort Hoyle, MD, on the Chesapeake Bay, was the one place I did thoroughly enjoy. When we got there I could ride my bike, shoot my BB gun, and pretend I was a frontiersman trying to avoid being seen by the Iroquois. Fort Hoyle had lots of woods, forest trails a bike could get through, and small clearings in which to put up my tent. It was a young boy's heaven. Mother would fix me a lunch, usually hot dogs, which I could heat over a small stick fire if there were no imaginary Indians around, otherwise I had to climb a tree to dine so that I would not be surprised by any fierce animal or human. In retrospect it is amazing the imagination of a young boy.

I was old enough by then to be allowed to accompany my father out on the firing range with the French .75s which were our standard field artillery cannon. A battery still consisted of four of these guns and they would line up axle to axle to shoot. The caissons would be pulled to the rear after the ammunition they carried was unloaded by the guns. The horses would be tied up well to the rear for they often shied at the report of the guns. The artillery pieces would then be fired one at a time and finally, toward the end of the shoot, they would open up simultaneously and continuously for about a minute. The noise was spectacular. The bonus was that we slept overnight in a big army tent, on cots of canvas that were as hard as rocks. However that did not keep me from sleeping like a baby. We ate our meals by going through a chow line. I thought this was real living. Years later, when I was in the active army, I used to wonder what in the world could I have found so charming about a chow line?

The older boys on the Post used to carve small wooden ship models, put a stick mast and curved piece of paper sail on them, and push them out to sail on the Bay. Sometimes they would let us pot-shot to see if we could sink them with our BB "gunfire". Though we expended lots of BBs I don't think that we ever did. We occasionally did bounce a BB off one of the crabs in the Bay, but it was well "armored" and hence was not affected by our bullets. Dad taught me never to shoot at a bird for a BB might kill one, so it was only the squirrels who were pestered by .BB fire but usually all we hit were their tails.

Close to Fort Hoyle was the Army's Aberdeen proving ground for some of the new weapons with which it was experimenting, and the Army's Chemical Center. All I remember about the latter was occasionally some very bad odors emanated from the direction of the center if the wind was a certain direction. The Center itself was off limits to children and so we never visited it. Aberdeen Proving Ground was another story. In it were some fascinating weapons to be seen. Dad took me on a tour one day to see our new tank and some half-tracks. These latter vehicles had wheels in the front and tank treads in the rear and thus were able to make a lot more speed on a highway than the lumbering tank. I asked why they called a tank a tank, and found out that in World War I when the British were first building such a vehicle, they did so at a factory that made tanks to hold liquids. To keep secrecy, the British announced that "tanks" were what was being made at this factory, and the name stuck.

Then my idyllic life was shattered. Dad received orders to go to Paris. I guess we were expected to be excited but all I was concerned about was whether I could take along my BB-gun. I had no idea where France was located but Dad and Mom sounded so excited that I finally got used to the thought. We packed away a lot of our things because we would be living in an apartment in France. Thus I parted with my BB-gun; never to see it again. All in all I didn't think this idea of going to France was so hot after all.

CHAPTER TWO

Situation - 1938:

Germany: Emerging as the key military power of Europe. Testing new weapons and the concept of "blitzkrieg" (lighting warfare) in the Spanish Civil War. Having re-entered the Rhineland and seized Austria, she is now poised for seizure of Czechoslovakia.

Italy: Building modern naval fleet. Invades Ethiopia.

Japan: Having seized Manchuria, her army is moving southward along China's coast intent on defeating China and seizing the East Indies.

Great Britain: Still in "appeasement" mood. Prime Minister Chamberlain signs "Munich Agreement" ceding Czechoslovakia and brags about "peace in our time". Beginning to build up the Royal Air Force with modern planes.

France: The threat of going to war over Czechoslovakia finally awakens France to begin rebuilding its army and calling up reserves.

USSR: Having purged most of his earlier generals, Stalin is now beginning to rebuild his army in earnest. Like Germany, he is using Spain as a testing ground. He controls or influences the world-wide communist party from Moscow.

United States: Nation still in an "isolationist mood." Armed Forces are small with mostly antiquated equipment and an outmoded air arm. Country still trying to pull out of the devastating effects of the great depression.

Balkans: Largely ignored by the major powers. Large unrest in most of the nations, particularly Yugoslavia which is on the edge of revolt.

1938 - Father

One year had passed since my father had entered the "L'Ecole Superieur de Guerre". Dad excelled at history, and thus earned quite a reputation among his classmates as a strategist. He understood the German sweep through Belgium at the outset of World War I, and admitted that the Maginot Line might have been effective back then. However, he also became convinced that, with the spate of new weapons being developed, the Maginot Line, while causing many casualties to the attacker, would probably be ineffective today.

He familiarized himself with the German campaigns in Russia during the first World War. He also studied the buildup of the German Wehrmach and Luftwaffe, and became quite fascinated with the idea of mobile warfare that the Germans were creating with their Panzer (armored) divisions and Stukas (tactical air support dive bombers). He began to send back reports to the War Department in Washington of what he perceived to be the weaknesses of the French forces. He felt their static defense posture would not prevail against a highly aggressive mobile force. These ideas, however, were not well received back home as the current thinking was that France, who had "won" World War I, was the strongest power on the continent. Even people like Charles Lindbergh could not convince America that the Germans were building a powerful war machine.

Our home in France was not all work. Dad decided that his family would see the country. Therefore he took us on trips all over the nation. We explored the Loire Valley, Alsace-Lorraine, looked at Brest and Brittany, saw the Basque country, and spent a summer vacation at Alp d'Huez near Grenoble in the French Alpine region. We learned to ski and to hike and to eat lots of chocolates. These trips, however, were not just for sightseeing. Dad was selecting places deliberately so as to get a sense of the French people and their preparation, both physically and psychologically for war. During this time Hitler's threats over Czechoslovakia and Mussolini's threats in the Mediterranean were front-page news in the Paris papers. As he studied the disposition of French forces and their slow call up of reserves, he became more and more convinced that the French army would never match what Hitler was creating in Germany. There were some French officers who were trying to prevail on their Government to modernize and mechanize the army, and some of the French elite outfits, such as the "Chasseurs Alpin", the French mountain troops, were coming up with innovative ideas. But by and large the

French posture was one of defense, relying heavily on the Maginot Line to stop any German attack.

At that time Italy was making its moves in North Africa and Albania. I would have presumed that Dad would have been very concerned about the Italians, who had a good army, a modern fleet, and a powerful dictator at the helm. I remember his telling me, however, that he was less concerned about Italy than Germany, even though at that time Mussolini was considered the greater threat. There was no Maginot Line on the French Southeastern border and throughout history armies had traversed the land between the Rhone and the Po Rivers; thus France might easily be invaded from Italy. His reasoning was that the French had a fair sized fleet and he felt that should it be combined with the British Mediterranean Squadron it could very easily hold the Italy navy in check, and thus block any Italian Army on the "Cote d'Azur" – the southern beach of France. Further the Italians were not developing their air power the way the Germans were.

His real concern was the lack of **will** of the French to engage in another world war. France seemed to be changing premiers every six months and was still suffering from the effects of the world wide depression. He discovered on these trips that, unlike the people in Paris, the people in the countryside seemed relatively unconcerned with the Czech crisis. Only the Jewish people were keenly aware of what was going on and had begun moving to the Americas in droves. Psychologically France was a defeated nation. World War I had been fought primarily on French soil, and for four years the area of the Marne River was devastated. Every now and then in the newspaper we would read of some French farmer who had blown himself up by hitting a mine with his plow. The French had not only lost a generation of men but had lost their martial spirit that had characterized them under Napoleon a century before. Daladier, the French Premier, seemed to have little impact on his people.

It was at the French War College that Dad began to seriously study the history of the "heartland" – Central Russia. He realized that almost all the land invasions across Europe had started from the heartland, and he was very interested in the fact that the French seem to always ally themselves with the Russians. He was impressed with the Balkan mountainous terrain which had kept most of these conquerors out of that region, and the role that the Danube had played throughout European history. The Rhine had been a barrier for invading armies from the days of Caesar; the Danube, on the other hand, had been a point of entry for invading armies over the years. He read "Mein Kampf" (Hitler's written plan for power) and began mastering some of the German language as even then he was beginning to feel that Germany would be the key element in another global war. He used to tell me often that the key to being a good intelligence officer was to think like the other fellow. This was the time he was studying and acquiring background to be able to do just that one year later.

Because he spoke French so fluently, Dad was often invited out over the weekends to picnic with his French classmates and their families in the Vosges mountains. There he discovered that the Maginot Line was a hollow shell, mostly unmanned, and certainly not stocked or prepared for war. He reported this to the War Department. The War Department would send this information to the US Military Attache in Paris, who would go to the French Army and ask for verification. The French manned and maintained for show about five miles of the Maginot Line; the US Military Attache would be shown this sector and then report back to Washington that the information it was getting from Major Fortier was obviously faulty. However, inasmuch as he was seeing it with his own eyes, Dad persisted, and thus brought on himself the ire of his superiors in Washington..

1938 - Son

The first thing I remember about going abroad was the thrill of my first ocean crossing. Ocean liners seemed very large and we had a good time exploring the ship as well as watching the porpoises and dolphins at play. Apparently we had good weather, as I do not remember being at all seasick. Every so often we would pass another vessel, particularly as we got close to Europe, and I began to realize how much ocean commerce headed for the ports of England, France and Germany. The thing that still stands out in my mind was the day that we passed an old four-masted schooner under sail. Even then there were still some of these old ships plying their trade. Everyone came up on deck to wave at the sailors, and they climbed the rigging to wave back to us. Our captain even blew his steam whistle in recognition. It was a magnificent and beautiful sight ... And the end of an era.

We disembarked at Le Havre and took the train to Paris. I had never been on a train before so this was a new adventure. The French trains had these little individual compartments so the whole family could occupy one compartment and still be able to stow our luggage in the room. My first surprise was when the conductor came around to punch our tickets ... he spoke in French. That had always been the language Mother and Dad used to talk with each other when they did not want the children to hear the conversation, so I was quite surprised to find someone else knew the language.

I can remember passing the little French towns and the beautiful hedgerow country that would later be such a hindrance to our armies after they landed on D-Day. The quiet French countryside, with churches always on the highest hill in the village, and Frenchmen riding bicycles with a long loaf of bread tucked under their arms, was fascinating. Normandy and Brittany were farming country and the fields were full of cows, goats, and sheep. Having seen the gigantic farms of the American mid-west, I was surprised at how small each French farm seemed to be. Most of the farm houses appeared to have thatched roofs and I can remember Mother remarking about what a den of insects the roofs must be. There was little hustle and bustle in the open farms and tree-lined roads, and I thought of how peaceful the countryside appeared.

Then my quiet countryside was suddenly contrasted to the pandemonium of the main railroad station as we pulled into the outskirts of Paris. Confusion seemed to reign, and people were shoving and bumping into one another. Everyone seemed to be shouting; a characteristic of the French I was later to accept as normal. Coming into a railroad station, past the train yards, made Paris look dismal, dirty and depressing. It would not be until I had strolled the Seine or the Champs Elysee that I would later see the grandeur that is Paris. My first impression was one of horror.

The first thing that struck me about Paris was the number of crippled men on the streets and in the cafes. In those days plastic surgery was in its elemental stages and so the thousands of casualties of World War I still hobbled around the city on crutches, missing arms and legs, with disfigured faces. Many sat on the sidewalk begging alms. I also remember that there were many more women on the streets than men. Only then did I begin to learn how horrible war is and how terrible had been the carnage of the "Great War". It had wiped out a generation of French youth and I was seeing the result. Later, when my Father took us all out for the dedication of the World War I US military cemetery at Montfaucon, I began to appreciate even more the men who had fought only twenty years before. We passed through some of the battlefields of that war and the landscape was still barren and there were still scars on the houses. We visited one of the trenches and even then I could visualize how horrible living conditions must have been with your feet in the mud and afraid to stick your head up over the trench wall.

Seeing Montfaucon was a shock. It was the first time I remember seeing a "field of crosses". Long lines of neatly tended crosses, with an occasional star of David, stretched as far as the eye could see. These were the Americans who would not come home. I remember one cross was simply identified as "unknown". Dad explained to me that many of the dead who were buried here were not identified; they had been blown to bits by artillery or mortar fire. The cemetery was beautifully tended and looked so peaceful. It was a very moving experience seeing the American flag flying over this huge cemetery. After the ceremony a bugler played "Taps"; I cried as the traditional three volleys were fired over the graves.

I suppose everyone who visits it sees Paris differently. My Paris was an exciting city of strangers. The massive cathedrals of Notre Dame and the Madeleine; the Trocadero, the huge war memorial at one end of the Champ de Mars; the Invalids, the tomb of Napoleon; and the Champs Elysee, the broad main street of the city headed by the Etoile (the equivalent of our tomb of the unknown soldier at Arlington Cemetery) all made a lasting first impression which many visits later in my life would never dispel. I learned to love the little butcher shops with their rabbits and other meat hanging on hooks outside the door while flies buzzed around, and the sidewalk cafes with their tables set outside. On each table were the usual salt and pepper, but also a carafe of red table wine And, of course, everyone was jabbering away as only the French can do.

While my sisters were enrolled in French schools, I was sent off to the American School in Paris. This was great by me because there were lots of pretty girls there, something I was just discovering in life. We took the usual eighth grade subjects but also had to take Latin. Our Latin teacher not only conducted her class in Latin, but made us do a play at the end of the year ... in Latin. The only good part about the play was that we all wore "togas", a sheet wrapped around us. The flirtatious girls learned to let their sheets fall open just a bit – proving what the Chinese women have known for years, i.e. that a twelve inch slit up the side of a dress is much more exciting to the imagination than the bikinis worn today.

I learned to travel by subway to the American School. This was great because it gave me the freedom to explore the subway system. When we left two years later I was a subway expert – could reach any part of town without getting lost underground. With its narrow streets and reckless drivers, Paris can be a most difficult city to navigate unless one is familiar with the rapid transit underground system known as the "Metro". It is an amazingly efficient and fast system to whisk people through the city, and if you knew its intricacies you could get anywhere in the city in very little time.

Our school had a large gym, something unheard of in those days in the French lycees. Thus we had a basketball team to which every boy in the school belonged. I can remember the coach's dilemma as to when to play each student, as most of us were terrible, but he had a policy that every student would play in every game. So he would put in his star athletes early and try to build up a sufficient lead so that he could then run in the rest of us without losing the game. I've often wondered since how many games I cost him.

The most fascinating aspect of the school, however, was the bilingual and trilingual student body. Many of the attendees were children of World War I unions between American soldiers and French women, which meant that most of my classmates were fluent in English and French, and many who came from Alsace Lorraine also in

German. As they talked to each other they slipped from one language to another without even realizing they were doing so. For example, the French quite often use the expression "N'est-ce pas ?" for which there is no comparable English phrase. So when, while talking in English, they came upon a point in their conversation where "N'est-ce pas ?" was appropriate, they used it … and then continued on in French. Later they may hit on a German word, in which case they continued to talk in German. It was very confusing to a fellow who only spoke English; at best I got about 50% of most conversations.

One of the joys of living in France was learning to drink wine at an early age. Of course it was heavily cut with water, but nonetheless we as children began to acquire a taste for wine. Each evening we would sit down at our dining room table and Mother and Dad would discuss the events of the day. Unlike today we did not spend much time reporting on our children's activities; that we had done with Mother earlier. Evening meals were for discussion of the weightier events that were taking place around us. Thus early in the game we three children began to get a feel for the historic times in which we were living.

Both Mother and Dad spoke fluent French. As I said earlier, from our earliest childhood I remember that when our parents wished to discuss something that the children were not supposed to hear, they spoke to each other in French. Until my sisters became proficient in the language they could get away with it. I will never forget the evening that our French maid poured the soup over my father's head. She apparently had done something that displeased him and so, in French, while seated at the table, he told Mother that the maid was an imbecile, incompetent, and a disgrace. He had forgotten that the maid's native tongue was French – thus the bowl of soup over his head. She stormed out, irate, while we looked on horrified. Dad was the head of the house; it never occurred to me that you could do anything disrespectful to him. I had a lot to learn about French women's temper.

The Czech crisis changed the atmosphere in France. First of all we saw Paris putting machine guns on the roofs of some of its buildings, and probing the night skies with searchlights. They had these listening machines that were supposed to tell them of the approach of an aircraft. I remember wondering how a searchlight on the ground could keep focused on a fast moving airplane, but it was always fun to watch when every now and then they would pick up a French plane in their beam. I also remember seeing my first French tank as it lumbered down one of our streets and stopped in one of the parks. It was sort of scary. Then there were the many uniforms of the French colonial forces walking the streets. Moroccans, Algerians, French Foreign Legionnaires, and other colorfully clad men, not to mention the French "poilu", were everywhere. Without question the scent of war was in the air, but I was too young to know what it all meant. I think my older sister did, but to Margot and myself we did not know what war would do to our playing ... and so we didn't think about it.

Each weekend Mother had the chore of bringing my sisters and myself to one of the many parks that abound in Paris, where I would sail my little sailboat in the fountains, and we would watch Guignol and the other puppet shows. Paris abounds in parks but most of the time we would stroll the one nearest our home – the Champs de Mars. It is a beautiful tree lined park, interspersed with pools and fountains, and filled with statues. As we walked through the park Mother would patiently explain to me, one by one, who all those statues were. Thus she introduced me to Napoleon's marshals, the nine muses, the key French generals of World War I, and France's many other heroes. Little did I realize that she was laying the foundation for her son's later fascination with military history.

She also had the chore of dragging her children to an occasional opera and thus began laying the basis of our later enjoyment of classical music. At the time I thought the opera was sheer torture. It was impressive, however, and people were always dressed up and on their best behavior. In retrospect I realize that my Mother was continuously coming up with new sights to see and things to do for her apartment confined children. Coming back to Paris over the years, I can still stroll through the Champs de Mars and name most of the people represented there by their statues. Interestingly enough in all this strolling through the parks I cannot remember ever playing with any of the French children. Certainly there were plenty to play with as the parks were full of nannies airing their charges. Whether it was shyness on my part, or lack of ability to speak French, I just don't know, but I never really got to know any of them.

During the summer we toured the Loire valley and its castles where I learned all about Joan of Arc and the assault on Orleans, Vauban's fortress construction, and the medieval military campaigns. It is hard to describe the impact that was made on my young mind by these castles along the river. With Dad as my occasional tutor I began to develop a real background on the wars of the Middle Ages and on the role of the

Monasteries in Feudal days. I began to learn about the struggles between the monarchy and the independent dukes, between the French and the English, and between the Church and the Princes. The Loire Valley is a beautiful sight. The majestic castles, each very distinct, stand out all along the river. I found most of the castles to be dank and dark, and could appreciate what must have been the difficulties of living in these places. The duke or king's portion was always ornate, beautifully laid out, and filled with fine furniture. The servants' quarters, the guards' barracks, and the other lesser figures' living areas were confined, cold, and spooky. Much has been written about these castles and many people have visited them, so I will not describe them in detail. Suffice to say that as magnificent as these castles appear to be, even the poor in America today live better and have more than royalty in those days.

Learning about the monasteries and the role of the monks during the middle ages was particularly intriguing for me. I had not realized that, without the monks, there would be no bible today. When you saw the painstaking way the monks had of inscribing and copying just one copy of the bible, which might take one monk his entire lifetime, one had to be impressed with these men's devotion to God. I came to realize that in the feudal wars the monastery became the sanctuary or safe haven for the many victims of those wars. They were the original hospitals and social services.

Dad also taught me a little bit about the importance of terrain on the battlefield and raised questions in my mind about the worth of static defenses. He pointed out how the Mongols, with no armor and only small bows/arrows, were able to use the speed of their ponies and psychological warfare to overcome fortified city after city. He talked about the Plains Indians and their small ponies leading the carbine-armed US cavalry on wild goose chases and then massing to meet Custer at the Little Big Horn. Thus later, as a cadet at West Point, I could appreciate General Patton and his American Third Army's sweeping through France after the breakout at St. Lo. Patton raced south and then, just north of the Loire River and keeping the river on his right to protect his flank, he turned East and drove toward the Rhine River at lightening speed.

After we had toured the Loire valley we headed west to the Basque country, which is unique in France. It sits on the border between France and Spain, but speaks a language that is strange to both countries. With their berets and quaintly painted fishing boats, the people of

Biarritz seemed a happy and friendly group, unlike most city folk in France. There Dad taught me about the Pyrenees – the range of mountains that separate France and Spain. He talked about the difficulties the Pyrenees had presented to Napoleon's armies and their logistical lifeline. He taught me how the Royal Navy was able to control the coastal roads and thus force Napoleon to move supplies through the mountains. He also showed me how the French and Spanish fleets decided to stop the British Navy by engaging them at Trafalgar. The battle turned into a great victory for Lord Nelson and the Royal Navy.

I think the trip that all the family enjoyed the most was the summer we spent at L'Alpe d'Huez. This small Alpine town, high above the city of Grenoble, was simply beautiful. High in the mountains the air was cool and fresh, the streams were clear and cold, and the panorama magnificent. Snow could be seen on some peaks; it remained there all year apparently. Unlike most French cities of those days, or American cities of today, the town was very clean. People simply did not throw trash around. Little gardens were tended very carefully for the short period in which they could grow anything. Most of our time was spent walking. I remember how rugged the French mountain people were; they could hike long distances, up very steep hills, and carry tremendous packs on their backs. From our home we could see people climbing up some of the stiffer mountains practicing for a climb up Mont Blanc. It was there that I first ran into a St. Bernard dog. These animals were famed for their ability to reach trapped climbers. They were very large dogs, but also very friendly. I also remember that there was one monastery high up on one of the mountains not too far away and occasionally we would see some of the monks come down to the village.

On one occasion I went on a picnic with my Father and a group of French Army officers to the Vosges Mountains. I thoroughly enjoyed this trip because when it rained we could take shelter in those huge concrete bunkers and empty pill boxes which stretched from Switzerland to Belgium … the famed but empty Maginot Line. They reminded me in some ways of the castles along the Loire river. They had towers every so many meters from which one could climb the inside stairs and look out over the terrain. In the summer they were very cool and thus a great place for the French officers to take their families for picnics. If they dined outside and it rained, they simply went into the Maginot Line to avoid the storm.

I loved running down the cement halls dodging the occasional dripping water, and peering out from the gun ports over Alsace Lorraine and imagining what earlier wars must have been like. I remember the lines of concrete in front of the pillbox that were there to stop any tanks from getting close to the pill box and throwing in explosives. Unlike my father, my young assessment of these magnificent tunnels was that they were virtually impregnable … but the same had been said about those castles on the Loire many years before.

CHAPTER THREE

Situation - 1939

Germany: Having seized Czechoslovakia, she now turns to Poland. Created "Danzig" crisis as excuse to attack Poland on Sept. 1, 1939, thus formally starting World War II. In rapid "blitzkrieg" she overran Poland in a few short weeks. Invited Stalin to enter Poland from the East and ceded part of Poland to the USSR. Begins U-boat war against Allied shipping.

Italy: Having conquered Ethiopia, she now attacks and seizes Albania across the Adriatic Sea.

Japan: Continues southward march in China; fortifies in earnest the Pacific Islands within her reach.

Great Britain   Declares war on Germany but unable to help Poland. Sends British Army Corps and Royal Air Force squadrons to reinforce the French along the Belgium line. Begins relentless sea hunt for German raiders and commercial shipping.

France   Declares war on Germany, calls up reserves, begins to man the Maginot Line and goes into a "defensive posture". Lack of action results in this period being called the "Phony War".

USSR: Enters Poland's east side. Seizes the three Baltic States of Lithuania, Latvia, and Estonia. Attacks Finland but thrown back with heavy losses.

United States: Becomes concerned over Japanese aggression and begins to place some restrictions on trade. Begins to build what would later be called the "Arsenal of Democracy". Remains isolationist.

Balkans: Begins to realize the threat that Germany, Italy and the USSR present, which results in vigorous diplomatic actions and treaty negotiations.

1939 - Father

The information that Dad was sending back from France about the Maginot Line should have alerted our War Department to the new world of war; instead they continued in their belief that the French Army was the superior army on the continent and that their defensive strategy would preclude Germany becoming any more aggressive. Further they had a hard time believing Dad's reports on French morale and lack of will to fight. Dad's repeated messages were not well accepted. Thus upon his graduation from the French War College, he was selected to be the United States Military and Naval Attaché to Belgrade, Yugoslavia. He was crushed and believed firmly that he had enemies in the War Department who were out to defeat him.

A more remote and unimportant job could not have been conceived of in those days. Dad had despaired that this might spell the end of his career. Back home the Army was just beginning to grow and finally officers were being promoted. New units were being created on the drawing board, and these would require staffing. Even if we never executed the plans on the drawing board of the War Department, he felt that his services could be much more practically used as military attaché to France, though he was too junior for the post.

At the least he felt he could be more effectively used in the War Department's intelligence section, though he realized that his thinking was unconventional and thus not likely to be warmly accepted in the halls of power. He could be an instructor at the War College, or perhaps teach at one of the other schools such as the Naval War College. Certainly there had to be some better use of his talent.

He perceived that being isolated in the "back water theatre" of the Balkans could do his career little good. Should Europe go to war, he was convinced at that time that the Balkans would play a very small or non-important role and that there was nothing that he could accomplish in this new post that could really help himself or the United States Army. He was greatly discouraged and he told me later that he had even thought of resigning at that point. However, with war coming soon, he accepted his orders … not knowing that he had thus created the opportunity for his later fame.

Moving to Belgrade was an interesting experience for us all. Going from a crowded apartment in Paris, we now arrived at a truly "foreign" country as we perceived it. However, we also went from the small luxury of a part-time maid in Paris to the grand luxury of a complete complement of full time help in Belgrade. Everyone had servants and Westerners lived in the nicest part of the city. Years later, when he was a general, Dad would remark that even at that rank he had not enjoyed the privileges that he had enjoyed in Belgrade.

Once Dad was in Yugoslavia he made a point of getting to know the German Military Attache, as well as the attaches of Britain, France, Turkey and most of the Balkan countries. He was never able to get close to the Soviet attaché. He took the time to explore the main rivers, cities, and mountains of Yugoslavia both to learn the topography and to understand a little better the various cultures that composed Yugoslavia. Although he was a Roman Catholic by faith, he cultivated the Serb, Greek and Russian Orthodox bishops and priests for he had learned that a considerable amount of strategic intelligence was to be had through these organizations, and these priests knew the tenor of the people in the different provinces.

Everyone in the American Legation (Embassy) was concerned about whether Yugoslavia could hold together as one country or whether the pressures of the conflicting cultures, religions, ethnic interests, etc. would result in a civil war. What probably held the nation together during this time period was the looming threat of a powerful Germany. However, within the country itself, there was much divisiveness that plagued the central government. Dad was involved with the Yugoslav army and was told quite frankly by the Serbs that should war come they could expect the Slovenes and Croatians to defect. This distrust within the armed forces affected everything they did from deciding who would get the new equipment to how they would train and where they would put their garrisons. Nonetheless Dad felt that with Serb leadership the Yugoslavs could still put up an effective defense. In this he was later to be proved wrong.

The Minister (Ambassador) and the rest of his diplomatic people in the Legation were watching the "Danzig Crisis" very closely, for all knew that sooner or later Hitler would go after another country. Hitler had publicly promoted the doctrine of "Lebensraum", which translated meant that Germany was too small for the German race and therefore Germany needed expansion territory. Many in the Legation thought that the expansion would move down the Danube, which meant eventually Yugoslavia. Even then overtures were being made by Hitler's diplomatic people to Bulgaria, Romania, Hungary, and Yugoslavia to consider joining the Axis pact.

Dad, for some reason, thought otherwise – that Germany would move east ... meaning Poland. Danzig had been declared an open port, but Hitler had secretly offered the Poles a deal in which they would surrender Danzig to Germany in exchange for joining the new Germany and thus becoming a power once again. This would also give them protection against the Soviet Union. Hitler felt that Danzig was largely a German city anyway and thus thought the Poles would accept this idea. When the Poles did not, Dad came to the conclusion that Hitler must be furious and that Poland would be the next target and that it would be soon.

His analysis proved to be correct. Somehow, in Belgrade, Dad got his big break. During the spring/summer of 1939, Dad picked up concrete evidence of the proposed invasion of Poland by the German Army. He never disclosed to me how he received this information; all I know for sure is that he immediately and excitedly dispatched it to the US War Department. They, in turn, checked with the other American military attaches in Berlin and Warsaw, who of course did not verify the information. Dad was crushed when he was told that he was not to submit further dispatches unless they could be verified: "No more rumors!"

The spring passed and the Danzig crisis became the paramount item on the European stage. Both England and France were reluctant to strengthen their bonds with Poland, but they were also determined to draw the line on Hitler's expansion somewhere. Hence they tightened their treaties that called for them to go to war if Poland was invaded. How they could help the Poles was a questionable point; but the time had come for resolution and they felt that taking a firm stand, publicly, would deter Hitler.

Dad and the other diplomats were not sure. They then began to think that the Polish crisis might also be a feint by Hitler to divert everyone's attention while the German army drove down the Danube. They alerted the Jugoslav government and thus they, and the other Balkan nations, started arming in earnest. The one thing they were sure of was that Hitler was going to make another move, but no one knew where.

Sometime in late August, 1939 Dad obtained the actual "order of battle" of the German army for its next campaign, i.e. the details of the German plans for the invasion of Poland. Once again I have no idea of how he developed this information and he never, never, spoke of his sources even in later life. He had convincing evidence of when and how the Germans would attack, but now he had a dilemma. He had been told to stop sending information unless he could verify it, and this he could not do from another source. He had been told: "no more rumors". He was pretty sure he had the real thing and time was of the essence. After agonizing over the decision for some time, he decided he had to act, so late in the evening of August 29th he sent a coded message to the War Department, through diplomatic channels, informing them that on the morning of September 1, 1939, the German Luftwaffe would bomb Prague and the Polish airfields, and then the German Army would cross the Polish frontier in two columns in a pincers attack. He did not receive an immediate reply.

Since he had been told not to send any more dispatches he was now afraid that having done so had cost him his career; lack of response was almost certainly evidence of just that. Nonetheless he was so confident of the information that he threw caution to the winds, got up his courage, and sent a copy of his message, by clear cable, directly to the President of the United States. Today, where the White House with its instant global communications is involved in everything, that would not seem to be an unreasonable thing to do. However in those days it was unheard of for an officer to skip channels and to send something directly to the President. He could expect repercussions from his superiors, but he didn't care – he had done his duty as he saw it and probably his career was over anyway.

Early in the morning of Sept 1, as the Germans attacked, the messages came in from Washington. First he received a reply from the War Department which had been sent the night before, informing him again that he was to "cease and desist" sending rumors. Apparently once again the War Department could not get verification from any other source. However later that day, when the news of the German Army's attack reached the President, Dad received from the White House a cable commending him with the words "Well Done". Needless to say he was elated. Then he also received on that same day a second message from the War Department that read, in effect, "please disregard previous message; continue to send vital military information". From here on out White House briefings by the War Department would contain anything of note that he sent. Thus his reputation as an intelligence officer began. Finally he had been proven to be correct.

He was later to write to his sisters-in-law: "I was now given the special mission of reporting on:

(1) Mussolini's intrigues in Albania and Greece, (2) Hitler's infiltration of Slovenia and Crotia, (3) Russian encroachment upon Bessarabia, and (4) Turkey's attitude toward fulfillment of her commitments to England. I was also assigned as ad-interim Military Attache to Greece."(4)

Unbeknownst to Dad his sending of the alert to the White House by clear cable would have major ramifications later. The Germans had agents who were reading all transatlantic cables and so they read his. It was through this means that the Germans found out who he was and later they were to put a price of 100,000 marks on his head that would severely curtail his freedom to speak with other Germans and their allied officers in Belgrade. He noticed some of their coolness but did not know, of course, that his message had been intercepted by German intelligence until later. He tried to continue his close friendship with the German attaché, but soon they "drifted" apart.

Dad had not only alerted the people back in the US; he also took extraordinary efforts to alert Major Colburn, our US military attaché in Warsaw, Poland. Dad never told me the details of how he did it, but apparently he was instrumental in getting Colburn and his wife out of Poland ahead of the German army. I would later have the pleasure on two occasions of serving under General "Big Red" Colburn at the end of the war. He was a most impressive looking general, a large man with red hair and a big red mustache. He was, in my opinion, a "model of a modern major general" (to steal a line from Gilbert and Sullivan.)

All during the winters of 1939-1941 Belgrade seethed with rumors of war. Dad discovered the flow of planes and war equipment down the Danube to potential German allies and thus began anew to predict a German invasion of the Balkans. He did not know that instead of the Balkans Hitler would plan to hit the Soviet Union. All he knew for sure was that unlike the first World War, this war would not start in the Balkans, but he firmly believed they would be heavily involved. He used to talk about the weakening of the Turkish influence that had been so prominent in the first war; now he saw the troubles of the area more in terms of the various alliances that all the major powers were trying to effect. In short he did not know how it was going to come about but he was now sure that very soon Yugoslavia, and the rest of the Balkans, would be in the war. The threat of Italy along Yugoslavia's Dalmatian coast now that they had seized Albania, and its possibility of invading Greece thus surrounding Yugoslavia with Axis forces, troubled him greatly. More and more the diplomatic scene became difficult. I remember Mother coming home from a diplomatic party and telling us about how the British, French, and other "allied" people gathered on one side of the reception hall while the Italian, German, and most of the Balkan countries representatives would gather on the other side of the room. The Yugoslav hosts at the party would do all in their power to get along with both sides. They were also very careful not to imbibe least they alienate one side or the other.

As the tenseness built up, the Legation began to destroy much of its files and records. Dad was asked to get rid of all papers except the code books and other secret material. The feeling was that the Legation might be bombed in any attack, and that any material that might be scattered could be picked up and used by one of the warring nations. The under-secretaries at the Legation, as well as Mr. Lane himself, our Minister, began to stock their homes with whatever they could get shipped from the United States. They did not want to be dependent on Belgrade supplies should war come to the Balkans.

1939 - Son

In the summer of 1939 my oldest sister returned to college in the United States with an aunt who had been to Italy. My younger sister, Margot, and I regretfully left France and proceeded to the Balkans with our parents. Yugoslavia was to be a very new experience as we moved from a small and confined apartment in Paris to a luxurious house in Belgrade. There, in addition to a lovely large house and private yard, we had a maid, Justinia, a manservant/chauffeur named Yosef, and a cook called Anna. As we had in Paris, each night we sat down to the dining room table and heard Dad relate stories of what was going on in the diplomatic world. I also remember that many times we would be in the living room and someone would ring the doorbell. We would answer it and, unknown to ourselves at the time, we would usher in an ambassador, or general, or bishop or some other high ranking dignitary. Later Dad would tell us who they were and what country they belonged to.

We had great dinners, as the cook was a real pro. She was a chubby advertisement for her own good cooking. I can see Anna now as she returned from food shopping and bringing home, dangling by their feet, several live chickens. With her ax she would decapitate the birds and then clean and cook them. A city boy at heart I suppose, I never quite got used to seeing my meal alive before I ate it.

Belgrade was a unique experience in many other ways. The first things that struck us were the beautiful Serb Orthodox churches with their almost Oriental look. They were wonderfully ornate and full of lovely icons inside the church. Their Orthodox priests grew long black beards and wore black clothes, so they could be spotted many blocks away. The Serbs gave great reverence to their priests and to their church. The language, of course, was impossible to read or speak. We had to look at the pictures in the newspapers to get any feel for the news. I always enjoyed something like the coca-cola ads; one could recognize a picture of a coke bottle anywhere in the world. When not driven by the chauffeur, we made our way through the city on old trolley cars that resemble those in San Francisco's today. Animals were everywhere as most transportation was still the horse cart. I have to add that the streets were often covered with droppings and one had to watch one's step as he proceeded. I suspect that there could have been several epidemics but the cold weather generally precluded the spread of disease.

At that time Dad rated, and received, a brand new American car. It was a 1938 Buick, which he received shortly after he got there, and it was something for everyone to stare at. Even the Royal Palace did not have anything like it. I remember he worried constantly about its breaking down, for there were, of course, no replacement parts in Belgrade in those days. However the car was to hold up well and saw him through his later travels with the Yugoslavian army before he finally had to abandon it. He flew two small American flags on small flagstaffs on the forward fenders so the car was quite distinguishable as it made its way through the City. It is a tribute to American automobile makers that it was as rugged as it proved to be, going up mountain trails and rutted horse-cart roads. Dad was very proud of it.

Because I could not speak their language, I never got to know the Serbian people. The few I met who spoke English were a warm and friendly group. When we were invited to a Serbian Orthodox service, such as a wedding, I recall how beautiful the services were and how dignified the Serbs appeared. They owned very little, but they were a very tough people. My father would tell me of their long resistance to Turkish rule and the fact that their national holiday commemorated a defeat rather than a victory. He told me of their mountain redoubts and of their long guerrilla warfare with the occupying Turks or others. He was convinced that they would fight if invaded. To me they appeared as just ordinary people living ordinary lives on a pretty meager income.

The countryside was lovely. The small villages, with mostly thatched roofs, reminded me of the villages of France. The main difference is that it seemed that the farms had much more livestock in Yugoslavia, and the town centers were less definable than in France where everyone sat at outside tables and sipped wine in the village square. As I stated earlier all transportation in the country, with the exception of the railroads, was by horse cart. There were very few trucks except for those in the Army. Unlike Paris, a city of many bridges over the Seine, Belgrade had very few bridges. Thus I can remember that at the head of each bridge long lines of horse-carts would appear during the day, each cart patiently awaiting its turn to cross the bridge. Obviously the drivers would dismount and chat with one another. This is the only place I can recall that Serbs congregated to talk. Unlike the French, they were not a talkative nation.

Because there were few children of my age to play with (or with whom I could communicate) I picked up an old Remington upright typewriter and taught myself to type. With my very poor handwriting I'll always be indebted to that ancient typewriter for teaching me the keyboard and thus qualifying me for the computer age. I wrote lots of letters to my aunts in New Orleans, and they saved these for posterity. Thus today I have been able to refresh my memories of many of the events in this narrative thanks to being able to re-read my old letters of the time.

In July of 1939 I was returned to France to go to a Boy Scout camp at Etretat on the Norman coast. There we lived in those thatched roofed cottages and ate delicious country fare. We were organized into troops and so, regardless of nationality, we got to become close friends with those members of our patrol. Once again the tri-language boys would be hard to understand when they went into French and German, but by now I was used to it in school and so I found myself beginning to speak a little of both French and German. As a Senior Patrol Leader I did a lot of instructing in tying knots, first aid, and the other things a boy scout learns at that age. Unlike Fort Hoyle, however, one could not light a fire or go out in the woods in most of the French countryside, so we tended to stay near the water of the English Channel.

We bicycled all over Normandy and Brittany, and camped out along the Channel beaches. We would build bonfires out on the rocks and sand and sit around at night singing songs and telling stories, or practicing tying knots or first aid. The beaches were rocky rather than sandy and they were hard to sit on, so often we sat up on the bluffs overlooking the beaches themselves. Little did I know then that these very beaches would later become famous during the Allied landings of 1944 as "Omaha", "Sword", "Gold", "Juno" and "Utah", and that we were sitting on what would be the German's main line of defense. Today a beautiful "field of crosses", American memorial cemetery, containing the bodies of so many of our men who died on D-Day and its subsequent battles is located where we used to sit and cook hot dogs. Those of the Jewish faith are buried under the Star of David, the remainder of the dead are buried under marble crosses. The graves are laid out in long lines and the cemetery is kept in immaculate condition by our American Battle Monuments Commission.

Normandy is beautiful country. Along the coast the fishing boats lie on the rocks half the time for when the tide is out the tide differential is so great that the water recedes far out to sea and the boats are left high and dry. Beaches may extend out a whole mile at dead low tide. Fishermen take the opportunity to use this time when their boats are grounded to repaint and repair the boats, or their fishing nets. The "bocage" country consists of small farms with very high hedgerows, built up over the centuries, fencing in each farm. These would become nightmares for the Allied Forces once they had landed on the Normandy beaches and tried to break out of the beachhead. The area is crisscrossed with small streams and hence there are many little bridges with small communities surrounding the bridge. These communities are typical small French towns with farmers bringing in their produce or livestock to sell, with bakeries emitting delicious odors, and with the usual shouting and bustle that earmarks the French.

Bicycling along the English Channel northeasterly, we soon arrived at Calais and there we could see across the channel to the white cliffs of Dover. Looking out over the channel I could conjure what it must have been like for the Duke of Normandy to ferry across his men and horses and to attack and defeat the English at the Battle of Hastings in 1066. Seeing how narrow the Channel is at this point, I could later wonder at the success of the German fleet that, in the middle of the war, broke out of LeHavre and raced northeast through the Channel to Germany without losing a ship to the British. I could also understand Hitler's reluctance in 1944 to commit his two Panzer

Reserve Divisions to attack our Normandy landings; he was convinced that the main American attack would take the shortest route from England, i.e. over the Dover straits.

It was a heady time for a fifteen year old! Little did I know how much these days would contribute to my later love of military history. One day my Dad came for a visit and took me to the port of LeHavre, and there, flying the stars and stripes, was a cruiser – the old *Marblehead* - which would win fame at the beginning of World War II by sailing half way around the world, to an Atlantic port, after being all but sunk by Japanese bombs off Java. It is hard for an American today, now that our country has been the world's greatest power for over fifty years, to comprehend what it was like to see an American flag flying from a vessel. In those days one rarely saw any evidence of the United States in France, and even less so in Yugoslavia. I thought *Marblehead,* which was only a light cruiser, was the most impressive ship in the world, a virtual dreadnaught. I fell in love with the Navy.

Then one day in late August the Scoutmaster at the camp called me to his cabin and told me to pack my bags immediately. He had received a call from my father who wanted me put on a train to

Yugoslavia as quickly as it could be arranged. If necessary I was to leave all my scouting gear, bike, etc. with the camp and get on the earliest train. I asked if any of my family was hurt and he said no, Dad just wanted me home. Even though we all knew war was in the air because of the German demand for the free port of Danzig from Poland, I, for one, had no idea what prompted my sudden leaving. Within two weeks, on September first, I would understand.

PHOTOGRAPHS

14.   Top: Lt. Col Louis J. Fortier, US Army with Serbian officers in Belgrade, Yugoslavia in 1940.

15.   Bottom: Lt. Col Fortier, US Mil. Attache, Lt. Col. Clark, British Military attaché, with a Serbian Officer during the German blitz of Yugoslavia, April 1941. Note my father's mud covered Buick.

16.   Top: British destroyer escorting the United States passenger ship *SS Washington* into Gibraltar after stopping it on the high seas. Photo taken by the author from the deck of the *Washington.*

17.   Bottom left: British marines at the rock of Gibraltar, with mail unloaded from the *SS Washington* on the deck, about to board the American ship to select certain people to take off.

18.   Bottom right: Author in his uniform as a Junior ROTC officer, New Orleans, LA, 1941.

19.   Article in the New Orleans newspaper during the Yugoslavian revolt, April 1941.

16

17

18

YUGOSLAV NEWS MEANS MUCH TO THEM

19

New Orleans States Photos.

UP BRIGHT and early this morning to catch the first news from Yugoslavia were L. RENSHAW, SOLIDELLE and MARGOT FORTIER, children of LIEUTENANT COLONEL LOUIS J. FORTIER (inset), military attache at the American Legation in Belgrade. Solidelle has been in the country since October, 1939; the other two since last May. Mr. and Mrs. Fortier have written that they will leave Belgrade for the United States in April.

N. O. Students Fear for Parents in Yugoslavia

Children of U. S. Military Attache There Hope for Safety

BY BEVERLEY COLOMB

Three young New Orleans students—two pretty girls and a handsome boy—are taking the startling news pouring in daily from Yugoslavia far more seriously than their fellow students.

For mixed with their elation over the Slav revolt, the trio

—Solidelle, Margot and L. Renshaw Fortier—feel a bit of apprehension as to what it might mean to their parents, Lieutenant Colonel and Mrs. Louis J. Fortier now in Belgrade.

Lieutenant Colonel Fortier is a military attache with the American legation in Yugoslavia where he has been stationed for the past two years.

When the situation grew worse in Europe last October, Solidelle, 19, came to America with her aunt, Mrs. Edmond LeBreton, assistant professor of French at Newcomb college, who was returning from a European tour. She entered Newcomb as a freshman.

Sister, Brother Follow

Her sister and brother followed suit in May when all Americans who did not have official business in Yugoslavia were ordered home by the embassy. Margot, 13, is a freshman in Ursuline convent, and Renshaw, 17, a senior at Fortier High school. They reside with Mrs. LeBreton at 3369 State Street Drive.

"We are plenty worried about mother and father right now since trouble is breaking out in Belgrade and it looks like it is going to get steadily worse. If we were only sure of where they are, it would be better," Solidelle said.

The last they heard from their parents was over a month ago and at the time Colonel Fortier

CHAPTER FOUR

Situation - 1940

Germany: Seizes Denmark and Norway. Overruns and seizes Benelux countries and France. Begins aerial attack on Great Britain. Intensifies U-boat attacks on sea-lanes to England.

Italy: Joins in conquest of Southern France. Attacks Greece from Albania but repulsed.

Japan: Continues brutal campaign through China. US cuts off steel exports.

Great Britain   Germany's forces, overrunning France, push British Corps into the sea – most of the troops rescued at Dunkirk. Churchill takes over as Prime Minister. In the fall "Battle of Britain" Royal Air Force pilots wreck such havoc on the Luftwaffe that Hitler calls off his invasion of England. British forces occupy Iceland and Prime Minister Churchill makes a deal with the United States for the latter to give it 50 old World War I destroyers in return for leases for bases in the Caribbean.

France   Overrun by German blitzkrieg and northern portion occupied. Lower half of France allowed to constitute a separate "country", called the Vichy French, to keep the French fleet from falling into British hands.

USSR:　　　　　　　Completes conquest of Finland. Joins Germany in conquest of Poland.

United States:　　　US at last awakening to threats on both Oceans. "Lend Lease", a law that allows the US to arm Allied Countries, instituted in Congress (passed in 1941). Began discussion of Selective Service Act to create draft in case of war. Begins building modern aircraft and re-arming Armed Forces.

Balkans:　　　　　　Kings and leaders of Balkan countries pressured by Hitler to join Axis or sign pacts that would allow Hitler to move troops and aircraft down the Danube. USSR still ordering communist parties in the various countries to cooperate with Hitler.

1940 - Father

In January of this year Dad was sent on a secret mission to Cairo (Gen. Wavell) and Beirut (Gen. Weygand) to determine the political and military intentions of the Allies vis-a-vis the Balkans and Italy. He traveled through the Middle East trying to get a sense of how the people there really felt. However, he would tell me later that the Middle East was so complicated ethnically, politically, culturally, and theologically, that he did not feel he was successful in developing much useful information. As we all know the same struggles remain today.

After two years in Belgrade, now Lieutenant Colonel Fortier had gotten to know all the key officers of the Yugoslav General Staff, as well as the other military attaches. With war having broken out, the role of the military attaché as a source of intelligence was vital to each nation. One aspect of the war that is generally not known to most Americans was that Hitler decided to eliminate, wherever possible, the United States military attaches. He considered them as spies for the British. He was absolutely correct – President Roosevelt was passing US intelligence to Prime Minister Churchill. Thus the Germans killed our man in Norway and shot down our man in Egypt.

In Dad's case they put a price on his head, as they knew he had alerted the US to the attack on Poland. They had intercepted and read his report to the White House by commercial wire back in 1939. The price was allegedly 100,000 marks.

As the German Army's panzer attacks, supported by Junker 88 dive-bombers, swept through Poland, and finally France, it became vital that the new American Army, which was just being created through the draft, learn something of the Nazi tactics and organization. Hence Dad was to spend the remainder of 1940 studying the battle reports and talking with the German and Italian Military attachés to assimilate all he could about the Axis forces. Having told the War Department about the German battle plan for the attack on Poland, and then alerted them about the weaknesses of the Maginot Line and Germany's ability to penetrate it, he now had established himself as a key first-rate intelligence officer. Never again would he be told "No more rumors."

Now he started receiving requests for more intelligence on all of Europe. Somehow he had established himself in a key intelligence center and his reputation was growing back in the United States. Requests came for more and more information. Dad was now asked to study the

Italian military structure and, to the extent he could, determine how successful was the Italian occupation of Albania. Later, in the fall when Mussolini would attack Greece, he was asked to follow those battles as best he could.

Inasmuch as the US Navy was small and with few officers to spare for the Balkans, Dad was asked to serve also as the US Naval Attache to Yugoslavia and Greece. Thus he spent a lot of time studying the Balkan view of the Italian Navy, and those small naval forces that belonged to Greece and Yugoslavia. The Yugoslav Navy was made up mostly of gunboats and was designed primarily to help partisan activities being developed along the Adriatic. Greece, on the other hand, was an important maritime power even though she was a small naval power. Greek ships moved a lot of the commerce of the world, and Greece had a disproportionate merchant fleet for her size. Dad enjoyed his trips to Greece that this duty entailed, and so did my Mother whom he took with him on several occasions.

When Italy launched its attack from Albania into Greece in October Dad took the opportunity to study even more closely both the Italian Army and the naval situation in the Aegean and Crete. Churchill had ordered General Wavell, the British

Commander in North Africa, to move troops onto Crete and to be prepared to go in to defend Greece. However, the Greeks did not need help and threw the Italians out within a month. This was not lost on my father, who studied in depth the Greek defenses in the mountainous terrain – the same kind of terrain as Yugoslavia.

On one occasion he took me, to Venice, Italy. I remember it was a very foggy day, and as we came out of one of the canals we suddenly came upon a group of anchored Italian destroyers. I took several pictures before Dad got the gondolier to turn back into the fog. Later I realized he had gotten the names and types of each of the ships. Outside of Venice still later we passed the brand new Italian battleship *Littorio*; it was a sleek and beautiful vessel with impressive armament. However, like so much of the Italian Navy, it proved ineffective during the war. I believe she was hit by the RAF at Taranto. I did not learn until later that the purpose of these trips, particularly those to Albania and Italy, were actually to study the Italian army as it had adopted much of the German organization and equipment. No American had seen a German Panzer division in action, so studying the Italians was the next best thing. His trip to Venice had been primarily one of seeing the Italian forces on the ground, not on the sea.

He also took me up into the Montenegrin mountains. Here the mountain men were even then digging caves to hide weapons, ammunition and other supplies in the case of a German invasion. They were under no illusions; they knew that the Balkans would be invaded by either the Italians or the Germans. They had had a long experience with the Turkish invaders and were very professional at forming redoubts or creating caches of supplies. Dad had gotten to know a Serb colonel by the name of Draga Mikhailovitch; together they toured the Serb preparations for guerrilla war. He was greatly impressed with the Serbs' attitude of resistance and their plans to keep on fighting from their mountain strongholds until they were wiped out. However Mikhailovitch warned him not to expect the rest of the Yugoslavs to hold together; only the Serbs would fight he said.

One night we had dinner around an outside fire and I watched a wild boar being barbecued on a spit. When it came time to serve, the headman plucked out the eye of the animal and offered it to my father. Apparently it is considered quite a delicacy and was given to him as an honor. Horrified, Dad turned the delicacy over to me and with a few looks that I could not misconstrue communicated that "my son would feel particularly privileged and honored to taste it". With that I gulped it down; but with the result that I have never become fond of raw oysters even to this day – they still remind me of my Montenegrin night. When he was offered the second one Dad diplomatically passed it back to the tribal chief saying something like "such a great honor should not be bestowed twice". There are times when bringing your teen-age son along on a trip can be most valuable.

With the Italian invasion of Greece war had come to the Balkans. For the next several months all of the Balkan politicians would be busy trying to negotiate their way through the maze of international politics. Alliances were written and torn up, treaties were proposed and accepted/rejected with great frequency, and every nation's forces were being built up for the war to come. British strategy more and more included holding on to the Balkans and thus the Middle East. Churchill would call the area "the soft underbelly of Europe" and try to persuade the United States to commit forces to this area later in the war. But overhanging the Balkans was the Russian bear. Stalin's army was the biggest in the world, and while it was not the mechanized machine of the Germans, it was still formidable. Since much of the Balkans was Slav, the USSR was presumed to be watching everything closely, with the idea of jumping in when it might be propitious.

During this period Dad also made another trip to Palestine and the Holy Land with Mother. Mother would later tell us of the thrill of walking where Jesus Christ had walked, and the sense one got of the nearness of God when one contemplated the events that had taken place there two millenniums before. But the trip was marred by local fighting; just as it is today. Nothing has changed in the long struggle between the Jewish and Palestinian people. However, in those days, it was Britain's problem and Dad met with the British field marshal in charge. He admitted to me later that he was unable to perceive any solution to this crisis, and he felt that the Axis powers were happy that the problem lay in the lap of Great Britain.

Now came an agonizing personal decision for Mother and Dad. With all Europe at war except the Balkans, there could be no doubt that war would come soon, and so Mr. Lane, our Minister, ordered that all dependents of the Legation (Embassy) go home. All of the people had diplomatic status; however my father had a 100000 mark price on his head by the Germans. Therefore everyone feared for Mother's life and possibly the lives of the two children. Mother decided to try to send the children home, but she would stay with her husband and suffer whatever fate befell him. Several other wives of the Legation decided to stay but most thought it best that they go home.

After much debate among the staff, it was finally decided that the eight children of the Legation, all between the ages of eleven and sixteen, would be sent home in a body together, with the idea of confounding the border authorities at all the borders they would have to cross. They would be followed by several wives. They decided that Fortier's eldest child, the oldest of the group, would take charge of the group of children. He was given everyone's passport and money, and then the group was placed on a train headed for Trieste. There were some long, anxious, moments for the parents until they received a wire from the Captain of the *SS Washington* that he had all eight safely aboard in Genoa. Once again, however, my sister and I never heard from our parents about their worries of the time.

Now began long correspondence between my Mother and Father, and the "Tantes" (Aunts) in New Orleans. Many letters revealed what a financial burden was now placed on Dad. He had one daughter in college, and two teen-age children who were boarding at his sisters-in-law home. He had to provide for their food, clothes, play money, etc. In those days the salary of a lieutenant colonel of the army did not go very far. Dad ended up going heavily in debt, but he was able to provide for us all. We, of course, knew nothing of the financial straits we were causing; like all good teenagers we simply asked for more money periodically. Dad and Mother did have the advantage, however, of distance and "lost mail". When we made a request that they could not or would not meet, they simply "lost" the letter somewhere in the chaos of Europe. By the time they acknowledged the second request the need had long since passed.

The difficulties for Mother and Dad, trying to be both parents and also representatives of their country, are pretty well summed up in two letters Mother wrote to my sister and myself on the same day a few days after we departed from Belgrade. Mother's letter to my sister Margot read as follows: "For the first few days after you and Ren left, Justinia (our housemaid) moped about the house anxiously awaiting a letter from you. Both she and I want to know all about your trip. Daddy said that he would have given much to be hidden behind a part of the station in New Orleans – to see your arrival. What a joy for Solidelle!" However

Mother's letter to me of the same date read: "Things are going from bad to worse around us. We were all preparing for the spring, but we might see bad times before then. Russia is going right through Finland; after Finland comes Rumania, complications with Hungary; Von Papen has left Turkey; Bulgaria is at Germany's beck and call; somewhere in the midst of all this is Jugoslavia."(5)

The remainder of 1940 Dad and Mother spent in apprehension of impending war. Conditions were best described in a letter I have that she wrote to her sisters:

"You have no idea how curious and how unpleasant it is to feel completely cut off from the outside world, as we in the Balkans feel. No letters, no newspapers, no magazines, no parcel post, nothing do we receive from the outside world. The price of everything is steadily mounting because, naturally, Germany controls the market and when stocks run out they stay out. We are living in a Europe completely dominated by Germany; even we in the American Legation know that whenever he wished to do so Hitler could have all of us or any one of us recalled – that would not hurt our feelings very much – but the force back of that is rather appalling. Right now I am writing this in the hotel salon, and I am trying to concentrate amidst four separate German conversions going on – the place is full of Germans. Germany has just forced this country to change its prime minister; also has decreed that all industries shall come to an end – more raw material for Germany, more imports from Germany, more industrial workers turned agricultural to raise food for Germany. Also complete demobilization since mobilization meant one good loaf of bread per soldier per day. Germany sees no reason for a Jugoslav soldier to have a loaf of bread which a German soldier could use.

Do not think our life is hard however, since the members of most of the foreign legations belong among the 'unemployed' – there are no means of communications with the rest of the world hence no one works very hard."(6)

For Dad and Mother it was now a time to wait and see.

1940 - Son

Having arrived in Belgrade with my younger
sister, I was at a distinct disadvantage in that,
unlike my sister, I had never really learned French
– the diplomatic language – and I had no ear for
Serb or the Slav languages. My sister Margot had
learned to speak French while in Paris and thus she
could go to a school taught by French speaking
nuns, but Mother and Dad had the job of teaching
me at home. Mother took on the bulk of the task,
carefully drilling me in the English literature that
she loved, and in the history of Mexico in the latter
half of the 19th Century … because that was the
only history book she had. I cannot remember my
1890 history of Mexico, but I still can recite
Tennyson's "The Charge of the Light Brigade",
Kipling's "Gunga Din", Gray's "Elegy in a
Country Churchyard", and the many other poems
of English literature that Mother taught me. I cried
over "A Tale of Two Cities" and thought "Lorna
Doone" was a flop. I never appreciated how much
I owe my Mother for whatever classical education
I received.

Mother, however, was not mathematically
inclined and since Dad was never available, it was
necessary to employ a math teacher for me. The
man selected turned out to be a white Russian

fluent in many languages but NOT English. As he understood his mission he was to teach me advanced college algebra, which is what a Russian student would be taking at my age, not knowing that I had never opened an algebra book. He obviously thought I was the dumbest pupil he had ever had, and hence he taught me by pure rote learning. For one agonizing year I memorized, in French, four academic years of algebra. Boy, how I hated him! The results, however, were to stand me in good stead years later when I entered the United States Military Academy. The professors could not understand how I could be a top cadet in mathematics and also be at the bottom of my class in Spanish at the same time.

Mother also insisted that I take piano lessons. Apparently I was a total disaster in that field. I recall trying to "make little hammers" out of my fingers as I was drilled and drilled on music. I had never heard of such things as "Etudes". To this day I cannot do better than "Frere Jacques". However, somehow I picked up a harmonica and, with nothing else to do, I learned to play it; not well but creditably. This was the extent of my musical training.

The children of the diplomatic corps played with each other at one another's homes, but mostly we had few friends. Thus Margot was my companion and soul mate – a role she still plays from a distance. Occasionally, however, youngsters of my age among the diplomatic corps were invited to the palace to play with Crown Prince Peter. I only remember one occasion vividly; the time I was invited there to meet two young princesses of Britain's royal family. I returned home later to tell my parents about all the fun I had had with Princess Margaret Rose ... but that I didn't think much of her older sister. Perhaps this explains why, over all these years since she has become Queen Elizabeth II of England, I have never received an invitation to Buckingham Palace.

Dad and I spent a lot of time sitting on the shore of the Danube and Sava Rivers watching the barges tie up along the riverbank. There was a lot of commerce on the rivers, but Dad would always single out one of the barges and would then tell me to go down and peek under the tarpaulins and tell him what was on the barge. Warily, I would do so, until some sailor shouted at me to "scram", when I would run back up to the safety of my father. What I saw were mainly airplane parts under the tarps. What I did not know was that Dad had made me part of his intelligence operation; the Germans were shipping fighter planes down the Danube to Bulgaria and Romania. I asked him why they didn't use the trains that went through Belgrade regularly. He explained that the Germans could hide their aircraft parts on a barge, and they did not have to declare the merchandize as they would have had to do if they had shipped them by rail. Apparently they were unloaded in great secrecy, at night, when the barges reached Hungary or Romania.

Now my parents were faced with a problem. My older sister had returned to the United States to go to college, but there were my sister, myself and six younger children still in the Legation in Belgrade. As the war raged throughout Europe and had come to the Balkans in the Greek/Italian fight, our Minister (Ambassador), Arthur Bliss Lane, and his staff were now concerned about getting the dependents out. Italy's attack on Greece through Albania had been stopped, but the Italians remained a major Balkan threat. The Germans were sending troops and planes to both Hungary and Romania. Everyone was concerned that Germany would attack in the Balkans which led Mr. Lane to suggest to all the staff that they make arrangements to send their families home.

One of the things that I remember best about Europe in 1940 were the thousands upon thousands of refugees who were fleeing from various countries. It had started with the Spanish revolution and was followed by all the other displacements created by the conquering German armies. Many roads were clogged with horse carts, people, animals, etc. all over Europe but particularly in those areas where there had been invasions such as Albania, France, and the Benelux countries. All these people were headed for whatever ports to find whatever ships could be located to take them somewhere else. This would affect our getting out.

While diplomatic immunity should protect the other families, the fact that the Germans had put a 100,000 mark price on my father's head made everyone concerned about his family. After much deliberation it was decided that the eight children would go in a group, by train, from Belgrade to Lubijana, then Trieste, and finally Genoa. Several of the mothers would follow and join them on the ship. As the eldest I would be put in charge. Today I cannot imagine my making a similar decision about a fifteen year old with a twelve year old sister ... but things were different in the Europe of 1940.

It was Dad's idea to send the children as a group, as he had seen the swarm of refugees that now flowed over all of Europe, and he had made the assessment that the one thing "authorities" hated to deal with was children. He was dead right.

As the oldest I had been given the eight passports. Dad also gave me very strict instructions on how to be polite to, but not try to speak with, the various authorities I might meet. So the eight of us took off by train and had an uneventful trip until we reached, and were stopped at the Trieste border. The border authorities tried to talk with me in Serb, Croatian, Italian and French, but all I could do was to act and be dumb (apparently it came naturally). The Yugoslav border patrol decided to dump us on the Trieste border group, and so they passed us through. On the Trieste side they too passed us through and sent us on to their Italian border.

At the next checkpoint on the Trieste/Italian border, we ran into our first real problem. The Italian guards didn't know what to do with us so they called their superiors. These authorities also did not know what to do and began by trying to tell me that my group would be put on a train headed head back into Trieste. I pretended not to understand. Then the officials debated for about a half hour, and made numerous phone calls, but they finally decided to pass us on through and sent us to Rome. This was the one point where I got concerned. Finally we arrived in Genoa where we saw the wonderful sight of a huge ocean liner with lights playing on the big American flag painted on the hull. It was the SS *Washington*. We got off the train and went to the ship and were immediately taken aboard. Apparently the Captain had been alerted by the US Naval Attache that we would be taking the ship. I guess I should have been scared during this trip, but fifteen year olds can lick the world and somehow it never occurred to me to be frightened. After all, I had navigated the Paris Metro system; what could be more frightening than that?

For me the cruise home would be particularly memorable. Shortly after we sailed from Genoa, in the early evening, the ship's captain alerted us to the fact that we were passing through an Italian naval squadron. It must have been somewhere around ten p.m. It was a moonlit night, and I will never forget how beautiful these ships looked as they cruised leisurely and sleekly through the water. They appeared new and they talked to each other continuously by blinker light. It was impressive. After they had passed from sight we went to bed.

At about three a.m. we were awakened by the captain's invitation over the loudspeaker to come up on deck to see an interesting sight. It was the pursuing British battle squadron. Unlike the new Italian ships, the British squadron, headed by the WWI battleship *HMS Warspite,* were old and squat looking and were heaving heavy water over their bows as they plunged at full speed in pursuit of the Italians. Apparently at that point the Italians had not yet discovered they were being chased.

It turned out that we were actually witnessing the opening moves of a surface battle in which the Italian battleship *Giulio Cesare* and cruiser *Bolzano* would each take a hit. The English fleet was very unimpressive but there was no question of their intent; they were there to fight. We sailed right through the British formation and I thrilled at the sight of a prospective sea battle ... and decided then and there that I would become a naval officer when I grew up. This battle would prove to be one of the few encounters between the surface ships of Italy and England, as the Italians would elect to keep most of their fleet confined to harbor.

Shortly thereafter, as we were sailing through the Straits of Gibraltar, two British destroyers came out and diverted us into the harbor. There we dropped anchor for about two hours while a detachment of British Marines boarded us and apparently searched the vessel for something. I saw them take off two people and what looked like several bags of mail. Then we were escorted back out to sea and passed through the straits into the Atlantic. As we entered the Atlantic our ship was lit on both sides to identify us as an American ocean liner.

A day later the ship stopped at sea and the Captain ordered us to lifeboat drill. We all put on our life preservers and went to our lifeboat stations. While there we were approached by a small boat, which probably came from a German submarine. Several sailors boarded us, and then they took off several sacks of mail and left. I never actually saw the U-boat, if that is where they came from, for by the time we were released from lifeboat drill there was no small boat to be seen, and if it had come from a submarine the U-boat had disappeared beneath the waves. We wallowed for a few more hours before the Captain picked up steam and continued on.

Finally we closed in on New York harbor and passed the Statue of Liberty. It had been four years since I had last seen the United States and it was a thrill to see her from the sea. Manhattan, with its tall buildings, can be seen long before one enters the harbor. As we made our way up the Hudson River tugboats pulled alongside, received lines from the ship, and began to jockey us into the pier at 42nd Street. It was at this point that I began to panic for the first time as I was not sure what we were to do then. On board ship I had given the passports of the other six children to the women who accompanied us; but I still had Margot's and mine, with no clearcut instructions as to what to do next.

Fortunately that problem was solved for me. An announcement from the bridge asked Margot and myself to come to a certain lounge and there we were met by State Department officials who assured us that our parents were okay. They then took us off the ship, cleared customs for us, and put us on a train to our next destination. In the case of Margot and myself, it was to our Aunts' home in New Orleans where we would rejoin my older sister.

Mother's four maiden aunts lived in a big house in New Orleans. Another Aunt and Uncle, and their children of our age, lived in the house alongside. For the next year my aunts and uncle would take care of us, board and feed us, and see to our schooling and growing up. We learned to love them all. My four next-door cousins took us in tow and showed us around New Orleans. One, a boy of my age, Maurice Stouse, became my best friend.

One of my aunts had a small bungalow in Slidell, Louisiana across Lake Pontchartrain. At that time this was very much rural country and my sister Margot and my cousins and I used to love to go over there. Along the bayous we could crab and fish, or catch turtles, or run from snakes. The deep woods and marshy terrain made every expedition down the road a real adventure. The one thing we learned was to always return to the house as evening approached; otherwise one would be eaten alive by the mosquitoes.

I think the thing that astounded us most upon our return to the United States was the complete lack of understanding, or even interest, in the events in Europe by the kids our age. Even our cousins, with whom we played daily, thought very little of Europe or our experiences. Margot and I learned to put it all behind us, as no one was the least bit intrigued as to where we had been or what we had done. Having left the war-torn atmosphere of Europe, we could not understand how little the Americans knew, or seemed to care, about what went on. They read it in their daily papers, but it meant nothing to them as they were not affected by it. Most children my age could not even identify where the Balkans were, much less where the fighting was raging or what had happened to France. Years later I would be very sympathetic to our fighting men returning from both Korea and

Vietnam who were struck by the total indifference of the American public. There is nothing like having a few bombs hit your city to wake you up to world events.

One group was sympathetic. In my high school class there were two girls who were refugees from Great Britain. When the Germans started mass bombing of English cities, many British families sent their children to live with American cousins or friendly American families. Thus I got to know, and like, these two English girls with whom I could talk about the events in Europe. I felt very sorry for them because some of my classmates thought they had been sent over to America because they were not very good students in England, i.e. they had flunked school. I regret that I can no longer recall their names, but I will never forget their faces ... nor their accents.

CHAPTER FIVE

Situation – 1941 (Jan-Apr)

Yugoslavia: Yugoslavia was created by edict of the victorious Allied Powers after World War I. They put under one government the various Slav kingdoms of Serbia, Croatia, Bosnia, Slovenia, etc. It was a mix of diverse religions and cultures, including Roman Catholic Slovenes, Orthodox Catholic Serbs and Montenegrins, Protestant Magyars and Bulgars, and Mohammedan Islanders. It was conceived as a federation but was set up as a kingdom under the Serb house of Karageorgevitch. The seven million Serbs represented less than half of its fifteen million people. King Alexander was put on the throne but assassinated in France in 1934. Inasmuch as his son Peter was a young boy, his brother Paul took the throne as regent. Paul was not only disliked by the country's minorities but also by most of the Serbs.

By March of 1941, Yugoslavia was on the verge of a civil war – a war between those who supported fascist Germany and communist Russia, a war between Serbs and Croats. The Serbs are people of strength, courage and patriotism, and they have a long tradition of fighting for their national honor.

Their fellow Slavs, the Croats and Slovenes, have a long tradition of appeasement, which kept them under the yoke of Austria-Hungary until 1919. Thus the Yugoslav Army of 1941 was a disorganized array of disgruntled groups rather than a tightly knit combat unit. Their decision to keep small ethnic units made up from only one area, rather than going to a full integration of the Army could mean the possible defections of large sections of the battle line should war come. Yugoslavia also lacked modern arms, equipment, tanks and planes.

1941 (Jan-Apr) - Father

During the winter of 40/41, Dad continued to provide for his children in New Orleans; writing us many letters to encourage us to write back. Both he and Mother admitted later that they did not have a lot of time to be worried about us; they knew we were well provided for and Yugoslavia was in turmoil. Mother wrote of the "freezing" of relationships among the diplomatic corps, and the hard time our Legation people had getting anything done through Prince Paul's Yugoslav government. Mr. Lane complained repeatedly to the palace, but his entreaties fell on deaf ears. That was all the convincing evidence that the Americans needed to know that Paul was going to side with the Germans. On March 26th Prince Paul, under heavy pressure from Hitler, finally signed over his country to the Axis. Hitler was jubilant and now he had all of the Balkan nations allied with Germany. Prince Paul returned from Berchtesgaden, Hitler's Bavarian retreat, knowing that his signing would not be well accepted at home, but he felt he had had no other choice. Germany had threatened serious repercussions if he failed to sign.

At 2:00a.m.on March 27th, General Dushan Simovic, the chief of the Yugoslav Air Force, led the revolt that overthrew Paul's government. Trusted air force and artillery units surrounded the garrisons, public buildings, and seized communications. Prince Paul and his prime minister were arrested, and King Peter was crowned as the new Yugoslav king. The American correspondents who were in Yugoslavia following and reporting on events besieged Mr. Lane and Dad. Cecil Brown, Cy Sulzberger, Leon Kay and Ray Brock had all become his good friends. Later they were to be frustrated by their inability to get their stories out; communications was poor and Yugoslavia quickly became a completely disorganized society. Dad tried to arrange the use of Yugoslav military communications for these correspondents, but to no avail. They didn't have enough signal equipment to operate their own army.

The Serbs were jubilant even though they knew they would be struck momentarily. Ray Brock was to write: "... celebration in Belgrade was the most heartfelt demonstration of pure joy and thanksgiving that I had ever seen."(7) while other correspondents would each send similar descriptions of the popularity of the overthrow. Leigh White wrote: "... Serbian peasants openly demonstrated against the old regime without any fear of consequences. On March 26th, the day after the signing of the Pact, revolts broke out in towns and villages all over Serbia and Montenegro ... It was a revolution of the Serbian national spirit – an act of faith and of loyalty to the peoples' forebears, who had fought for centuries to win their independence from the Turks."(8)

Minister Lane was to describe the resulting scene as follows: "On March 27th, 1941, shortly after 2:30a.m, Mr. Ray Brock, correspondent of the *New York Times* in Belgrade, telephoned me that a 'state of siege' had been declared and that all telephone communications in the city had been cut. He had contrived, however, to reach me on the one line that had not yet been suspended. Immediately after giving me this warning, that line was broken. I dressed hurriedly, requested my chauffeur to do likewise, and set forth in the automobile for the center of the city. We were unable to proceed by the usual route as all the main arteries were blocked by tanks. By 3:30 in the morning many American newspaper correspondents had come to the Legation. They, like ourselves, were in doubt as to whether a coup d'etat had been effected or whether the Government was taking steps to prevent a move against it. Our military attaché, Lieutenant Colonel Louis J. Fortier, and I then proceeded towards the War Ministry, but were stopped two blocks away by a tank and a detachment of soldiers armed with machine guns. Fortier made his identity known and asked to see the officer in command. We waited some ten minutes before a youngish officer approached and with great emotion embraced Fortier. He then drew himself to attention and said to me in a voice vibrant with feeling, 'I salute you in the name of His Majesty, King Peter II, who ascended the throne of Yugoslavia at 2:20 this morning.' '... The coup d'etat was so skillfully executed that only the actual participants were aware of its preparation.'"(9)

Our Ambassador would go on to state: "As soon as word of the coup d'etat was known, Yugoslavian, and even old Serbian flags, were displayed on almost every building. Crowds of shouting, almost delirious peasants marched through the streets singing patriotic songs and shouting, 'Down with the pact' and 'Better war than pact.' ... The early morning crowds shouted that we should raise the American flag over our building, but I hesitated to do so until I ascertained the real meaning of the coup d'etat. When we learned that a national holiday had been declared and that all Government buildings were flagged, I gave orders to raise our flag. This action was greeted with great enthusiasm by the crowd which massed outside the Legation."

Knowing that this meant war in Yugoslavia, and with his children already safely returned to the

United States, Dad now had to think of Mother's safety. He would have to go out in the field with the Yugoslav army if Germany attacked; Mother could not accompany him. They did not feel it was safe for her to stay in the Legation if Germany overran Belgrade. So, on Saturday, April 5th, Dad now dispatched my mother, by train, to the Italian frontier knowing that Hitler could attack momentarily. On Palm Sunday, April 6, 1941, Von Kleist's panzer army invaded Serbia/Croatia and started their stuka bombing attacks on Belgrade and on all transportation centers. Von Weichs' Second Army followed up and seized all the key towns, road junctions, and vital installations; and took the defecting Slav groups as an adjunct to his army.

Mother did not make it. Just outside of Lubijana, Mother's train was bombed and the engine wrecked. Everyone was ordered off the train, but after several hours many of the passengers re-embarked since there was no place else to go. Shortly thereafter the train started moving backwards to the last town they had been through … and then stopped dead. The engineer announced it would go no further and again ordered everyone off as the cars were being seized by the Yugoslav army for the transportation of troops. Mother was now on her own, a solitary refugee in a torn land.

Thus began an incredible, one-week, trek back to Belgrade which Mother made by walking, riding on the back of an oxen team, and hitching a ride with a fleeing and drunken soldier in his broken truck. She had first tried to get help from the nearest military facility, but the commander told her flatly that no help was available. She then rode on a peasant's ox, and finding that too hard, hiked many miles to another military facility where apparently the commander helped her out by putting her in a truck that was headed toward Belgrade. This driver took her a short distance and then told her to get out, as he was not going to Belgrade, he was defecting. Not speaking the language (but speaking French and a little German), Mother finally found a drunken soldier in a truck who apparently was also deserting. He drove her the rest of the way. Mother was a woman of iron will and I suspect she scared the driver more than he scared her. We still do not know all the details of how she made it back; all I do know is she arrived at the US legation in Belgrade on Easter morning. Finding the legation smashed, she then cajoled the drunken deserter to drive her to the residential area outside of Belgrade where our first secretary, Mr. Robert B. Macatee, Commercial Attache Carl Rankin, and Second Secretary Bonbright all had their homes. Sometime late that morning she arrived at Dedinje and there found Mr. Lane and the entire Legation staff at the Rankin house …with one exception. The only one not accounted for was my father.

Mother was one of these individuals who do not display their emotions. As a result, in the retelling of this tale to her children she never dwelt on the fears and concerns she must have had during this terrible week. She had to have been frightened by the bombed train and being in the middle of a country in which she not only did not speak the language but was also married to a man with a price on his head. She was gifted with remarkable practical determination and she was going to continue striving to reach Belgrade in any way whatsoever. Finally, when she reached Mr. Rankin's house and found the Legation people had no word on her husband, she had to have feared the worst – that he had been killed or captured. It was an agonizing week for her.

Dad did know the time of the German attack. Leigh White wrote: "… The lights came on again and Ray Brock put in a call to Colonel Fortier's home. This time Lou Fortier was at home but Brock said he seemed annoyed at having been disturbed. 'Go back to bed', he said, 'If anything happens I'll let you know'. He later told me that he had been in uniform as he said this and had been up all night burning secret papers at the Legation. The General Staff, he said, had warned him that war would probably start at dawn, but had pledged him to secrecy and so he had not seen fit to impart this knowledge to the press."(10)

Dad had joined the Yugoslav army in the field and watched the defections of the non-Serbs cause the army to fall apart. General Simovitch and his staff established their headquarters at Banya Kovilyatcha in Central Serbia. Dad arrived there with correspondents Kay and White to find that Simovic had lost all of his communications. However, the British legation had a portable radio operated by the military and naval attaches (Col. Clark and Capt. Despard). For the next few days this radio became the one means of communication between Simovic and his field units but the latter were being decimated by the German armored columns. By April 9, General Simovic decided the war was lost despite protestations from Dad and his British colleagues. The general advised the three foreign officers to take off their uniforms lest the German take reprisals on them, but they refused to do so.

Once he realized that the Yugoslav army was folding, Dad recognized his duty was to study all that he could about the German blitzkrieg tactics which had become the scourge of Europe.

So he took his black Buick, with its little American flags on the fenders and proceeded to fall in behind one of the Panzers. At last he would see one in action; no longer need he study the Italian Army – now he would see the real thing. Trailing behind the German Panzer Division, he learned its strength, composition, organization, and deployment tactics, and how it refueled itself from its tanker trucks that followed behind the tanks.

He did not worry about gas for himself. He knew enough about the psychology of a disciplined German soldier to know that he could drive up to a German gasoline truck in his American officer's uniform, shout "Achtung" and demand that the German private fill his car with gas and that the private would obey, because German soldiers in crack Panzer divisions obeyed officers. Apparently he got away with this twice. Thus, for at least one day, he trailed and watched the Panzers in action.

After a day, however, Dad realized that he could not keep this up; he was bound to be reported and word would reach higher authority about this mysterious black Buick, and so that night Dad turned around and took off for Belgrade. For a short time he was pursued by German MPs on motorcycles but soon they were recalled. The next morning, however, he started down mountainous roads only to be greeted by fire from

German Messerschmitts sent to take him out. For a period of better than one hour two fighter planes kept diving on his car each time it would be exposed to the aircraft as it went around a mountainous bend in the road. It was a game of cat and mouse; he had to time his runs on the exposed side of the hill very carefully. Miraculously, though the car was riddled with bullets, Dad was never injured. To this day the family keeps as a souvenir of the incident a torn and bullet-ridden fender flag that Dad brought home with him.

Having the intelligence he needed on the Panzer division, Dad continued to proceed to Belgrade. On the way he picked up Cecil B. Brown, the CBS radio war correspondent. In his article in the *Saturday Evening Post* Brown relates what happened next:

"Our objective was to meet the German attack head-on, penetrate the Nazi lines and somehow thread-needle our way through them to Belgrade. Fortier hunched over the wheel, eyes peeled for the telltale fresh patches in the road that would indicate mines. Learning the Nazi troops were not far off, we pulled to the side of the road to wait for the Germans. Colonel Fortier, in uniform, sat behind the wheel. We grasped our door handles. Fortier tugged at his Army cap, setting it more firmly on his head. We grinned at each other, not a wide grin, but it would do. Fortier took up a can of cigarettes.

We didn't have long to wait. Four motorcycles, each carrying three German soldiers, roared up and screamed to a stop, forty feet from the car. In a jiffy the 12 Germans were charging at Fortier and myself, some with tommy guns, some with rifles coming up to their shoulder, and some with hand grenades ready to let go. We jumped from the car and yelled in German: 'Amerikanische ! Amerikanische !'

As they bore down on us we advanced towards them shouting we were Americans and then Fortier persuasively called out 'Have an American cigarette.' That stopped the Germans cold. They not only took an American cigarette; they took the whole can. Then they borrowed some gasoline, giving Fortier a note to some troops 50 kilometers back, for repayment of the gasoline. The 12 Germans astride three motorcycles were the advance point of the German Army ... and Col. Fortier and a can of American cigarettes held up the blitzkrieg for fifteen minutes."(11)

The article goes on to say that they pushed on when the Germans left and soon ran into, and were arrested by, a Croat in German uniform – one of the many deserters and fifth columnists in the Jugoslav army. A little later the blitz arrived. Brown goes on to state: "Around the bend we ran smack into the Wehrmacht – the first of a seemingly endless stream of mechanical monsters that is the German Army. In the three-hour ride – a matter of 40 to 45 miles, we breasted two Panzer divisions and one motorized division." Later, when the German commander had released the two of them and sent them on their way to Belgrade with a pass, they moved on, with a German corporal at the wheel – "one lone car bucking the German advance and that car flying the American flag".

Dad arrived in Belgrade the morning of Easter Sunday. When he arrived he saw that the Legation had been bombed and deserted. The Germans had been very systematic in their Stuka bombings, taking out the power station, the water supply, selected military targets and our Legation. He arrived at the abandoned and flattened building to find the Embassy's second secretary, who was a Texan, lassoing champagne bottles from the cellar through a broken window at ground level. Since Belgrade's water supply had been hit by German stukas the staff were bringing champagne to their residence where they used it to drink, cook, brush their teeth and even bathe and wash clothes. Years later Mother would still never touch a drop of champagne … and she lived to age 94.

After Dad had inspected the bombed Legation building he drove out to Mr. Lane's house. He found the residence all but destroyed. A bomb had obliterated the house next door and carried away a part of the Lane home as well. There were no signs of life, so he decided to drive out to Dedinye, where many of the Legation staff had their homes. He had no more than driven up to the Rankin house when he saw a woman getting out of an old army truck …

… It was my Mother.

Thus they were reunited, each having had an incredible adventure, but both having had no idea of how the other had fared. Once again neither of my parents shared with their children what must have been their astonishment, delight and relief upon seeing each other. I can only imagine what torture they had both undergone during that time thinking of the fate of the other, and thus what ecstasy they must have felt upon being reunited. However, we can only surmise; they never talked about it.

Dad then reported to Mr. Lane and told him that he felt "the jig was up". After lengthy discussion, Dad elected to go back to Simovic's headquarters at Kovilyatcha. Mr. White then tells the following story: "On our way back ... with Fortier, we stopped at an airdrome near Valyevo to ask about the progress of the war. It so happened that the bomber squadron on the field was commanded by an old friend of Fortier's, a colonel who, like Lou himself, had been educated in Paris at the Ecole de Guerre. The colonel and his pilots were having dinner when we arrived and they invited us to join them. We dined on pita, and musaka, a sort of hash combined with eggplant and covered with cream sauce. Both had been prepared by an army cook who would have qualified as a master chef in any capital of the world. ... Fortier, Kay and I were very hungry and we consumed our meal with relish, to the great enjoyment of the jovial cook who kept filling our glasses with wine. But I noticed that the colonel and his pilots had hardly touched their food. Fortier was a native of New Orleans, a dark, slight, jovial man with a gray mustache and a pleasant southern drawl. He was always in good humor. Even now he found it difficult not to be cheerful and he smiled at his friend, the colonel, as he finished his musaka. The colonel smiled wanly in return and poured himself another glass of wine. After complimenting the chef in Serb-Croat, Fortier turned to the colonel and said in French: 'Well Milan, how is it going ?' 'Nous sommes foutus', the colonel said. 'Not yet Milan' protested

Fortier, 'the war's only beginning. A lot of things can happen yet.' 'The war's over for Yugoslavia ...' replied the colonel '... We'll go up and drop a few bombs and be killed for our pains. But a lot of good its going to do ! Yugoslavia's done for – absolument foutu'"(12).

Dad, realizing the hopelessness of the situation, returned to Belgrade. As he said goodbye to the two correspondents who had been with him he asked Leigh to do him a favor. "Leigh,' he said, 'You know that I've got three kids back in New Orleans. They're probably a little worried. If you're ever able to get a story out will you mention that Solidelle and I are well and happy – and that we send our best to the kids?'"(13)

1941 (Jan-Apr) - Son

The spring of 1941 was a glorious time. My sisters and I were living with my Mother's maiden sisters in New Orleans. Because I had had no high school, the public school authorities were at a loss to decide where to put me when I first returned. Hence the summer of 1940 they had decided to give me a math and social studies test. The social studies test was centered on the events in Europe so I passed that one with flying colors. Fortunately, for math, they gave me an algebra test ... that promptly landed me in the senior class. In fact before the spring was out, I had represented my school at the Louisiana State Academic Olympics in algebra. I may have learned it by rote and in French but it stuck with me; I was considered a very advanced student.

By coincidence the nearest high school to our house was the Alcee Fortier High School, named after a great uncle of mine, so later, when I was made the commander of the fledgling army junior ROTC unit, I always suspected it was because of name recognition rather than any talent on my part. Fortier High was, at that time, a relatively new school and we were busy building up our football team (a big sport in New Orleans) and school spirit. Thus the little Junior ROTC had lots of marching to do during the halves, and we spent a lot of time on close-order drill and the manual of the rifle. In retrospect playing toy soldier was a lot of fun and probably good training for the future.

As the situation in Yugoslavia, from the overthrow of Paul's government to the subsequent invasion and overrunning of the country by the Nazis, made headline news, my sisters and I were suddenly VIPs for the press. I remember being interviewed to "tell us what it was like to live in war-torn Europe", and "How did we feel about our parents being over there." I would love today to remember what we told them but I cannot; however I do remember that I was very popular in school that year because of the furor. The press did a lot of speculation about Dad, a native son, in his role as Military Attache, and printed background stories about him. Hence we were often asked by our aunts' friends and our teachers to "tell us a little about the war in Europe."

Unfortunately, for about a month in the spring when the German's invaded Yugoslavia, we received no news about Mother and Dad. All news sources were dead, and the diplomatic channels had been severed. Later we were to learn that Dad had asked Cecil Brown and several other correspondents to get word to us about their condition; however, none of these people could get a line to the United States to file their stories or to pass to us the information on our parents. As diplomatic sources were cut off, and even the embassy in Rome was not sure where my parents were or what condition they were in, we began to worry about them. It was not until they actually arrived back in New York that we were alerted by the State Department who called us in New Orleans. From then on there was lots of preparation for, and anticipation of, their homecoming.

The big fun in New Orleans was that I now met something which I had just begun to discover in Paris and didn't have a chance to meet in Belgrade, namely girls!! In the war torn Balkans, a fellow who couldn't speak any language but English didn't have much chance of meeting girls. Fortunately, in New Orleans, my cousin Maurice Stouse, was a hit with the ladies; hence I met many girls in school. I might also add that the Junior ROTC uniform looked very impressive to the ladies (or so we thought). It was a great time.

During the previous summer we were deprived of this aspect of our career when my aforementioned cousin, Maurice, and I were sent to Port Arthur, Texas to be supervised by another much older first cousin. My Mother had been one of thirteen children, and the oldest, Tante Marie, had had three boys of whom the eldest, Harry, was Mother's age. Cousin Harry was not only a Catholic priest but he was a Monsignor used to working with teenage boys, which meant that he demanded (and got) complete obedience. However it was still a fun time as he took us to visit the Alamo and the shrine to Sam Houston, and taught us a little about that part of the country and a great deal about Texas history. He reminded us that not only had our home town of New Orleans served under many flags but that Texas also had been both Mexican and American, and even at one time a separate nation with its own flag.

He tried to inculcate into us some theology and sense of charity. We worked with him distributing food to the poor and helping out some of the parishioners who would seek his aid. I realize he taught us by the simple technique of having us doing things. Once he had taught the two of us to be altar boys we served Mass with him every morning. (I don't think I have ever been as holy since.)

Then came the big disappointment in my life. Having remembered the Italian and British fleets that we had passed through on the voyage home, I still had visions of commanding a fleet of US warships at sea. Hence I applied to enter the United States Naval Academy at Annapolis. I had both the grades and the ROTC background; and thanks to Cousin Harry was in pretty good physical shape. I thought it would be a cinch. However, it was not to be. When I took my physical I was turned down because of my vision. In those pre-radar days, 20/20 vision was an absolute must for anyone trying to identify an enemy ship at sea. With 20/30 vision in one eye I was close … but not close enough. Even though my vision was correctable I was turned down for an appointment. Crushed, I decided to become a doctor.

CHAPTER SIX

Situation – 1941 (May-Dec)

Germany: Seizes Yugoslavia and Greece in preparation for attack on the Soviet Union. Attacks Russia, sweeps through western Russia by passing key strongholds such as Stalingrad, and reaching gates of Moscow before being stopped by cold weather. The six weeks delay of attack on the Soviet Union, caused by the Yugoslavian campaign, may have saved Moscow from capture that first year.

Italy: Attacks on Greece unsuccessful until German forces moved down to seize Yugoslavia/Greece/Crete. Forces in North Africa, reorganized under German Field Marshal Rommel, drive British into Egypt all the way to El Alemain before running out of supplies..

Japan: When United States cut off oil in fall, attacks the US naval base at Pearl Harbor, Hawaii. Seizes Indo China, Wake Island, Guam, Singapore, and invaded the Philippine Islands.

Great Britain   Desperately   fighting   off German U-boat attacks. Fighting delaying battles in North Africa. Loss of Singapore and two major battleships difficult blow.

USSR: Large sections of Russia fall to German army. Russian forces fight delaying withdrawal to Moscow; saved by severe Russian winter. Soviets order communist parties throughout world to take up arms against the Axis powers.

United States: Passed   Lend-lease   and Selective Service acts. Jointly occupied Iceland with Great Britain. Ordered "shoot on sight " policy against Nazi U-boats and began guarding convoys to UK and USSR. Struck by devastating aerial attack at Pearl Harbor and landings on Luzon in the Philippines forcing retreat of our men there to Bataan and Corregidor. Churchill and Roosevelt meet for "Atlantic Charter" which would give priority to European theatre.

1941 (May-Dec) – Father

When Dad returned to the Minister's house with Mother, Mr. Lane informed him that the Bulgarians were systematically bombing Belgrade even though it had been declared an open city. Apparently after the main German army had already passed through, their allies, the Bulgarians, had taken the opportunity to avenge themselves on the Serbs. (Even today Americans have a hard time trying to understand the ethnic and tribal hatreds that poison the Balkans.) Much of Belgrade had already been flattened by the German army going through. The bombing appeared pointless and did nothing but kill a few Serbs.

The Diplomatic Corps decided that they had to act. Hence they had prepared a letter, signed by all the foreign ambassadors, to the German high command to request the cessation of the bombing. Mr. Lane apparently asked Dad how the letter might be delivered to the German Commander. Dad is alleged to have said to Mr. Lane: "That's easy. I have a price of 100,000 marks on my head; let me take it, get captured, and I will be delivered to their top officer." Apparently, the ambassadors debated that solution for some time and the

Brazilian ambassador was so impressed with Dad's courage that he later put him in for the Brazilian Medal of Honor.

With that Dad took the letter and began by driving through the war torn battlefield to try to reach a crossing into Romania or Hungary. (The German High Command for this battle was in Hungary.) He had a remarkable three-day adventure. He decided to risk going through areas where artillery was falling as he could be reasonably sure that the infantry of either side would not be there; hence he could avoid being taken prisoner by low level units of either side. Finally his overworked Buick gave out. When he could no longer drive, he abandoned his car and walked, once again following the devastated area in which shells were still falling.

"Morning found Fortier safely past the German lines; but weary, wary, unsure of directions. For a long time he made his way through the hilly country, on the lookout for German and Hungarian military. To be halted by them, he knew, meant being taken to some minor headquarters where he would be delayed hours, perhaps days, while death continued to rain on Belgrade." He obtained an old horse. Then "for two days he jogged north … getting meals as he could from the robbed, hungry peasantry. Then at nightfall ... he found himself at the bank of the Draca River that divides Yugoslavia from Hungary." (14)

Wandering along the quiet bank, he discovered a leaky rowboat. He turned the horse loose on the bank; there was no way he could get him across although he knew how much he would miss the old animal. He then stepped into the boat and rowed himself across. Having arrived in Hungary he now had to keep hidden from everyone until he could reach his goal. He was exhausted, cold, and just about spent; he had gotten to a point where he thought he could go no further. Finally he took refuge in a mud hole along a railroad track and fell asleep. He has no idea how long he slept, but when he woke up and looked up from the mudhole, he spied a railroad handcar. Apparently the crew using it were taking a nap on the other side of the tracks. He jumped up and with strength even he didn't know he had, he finally got it started, with the crew running behind trying to catch him. He then pumped his way through further artillery fire on a railroad handcar, slipped through the various German positions, and finally got himself captured by German MPs at the German headquarters. He was shot at several times, but apparently had a remarkable ability to never get hit; quite fortuitous from our point of view.

Once captured he demanded he be brought to the German 2nd Army commander, and so he met Colonel General Von Weichs. When he was brought into Von Weichs presence he handed Von Weichs the Diplomatic Corps' letter. Von Weichs read the letter, laughed, and is alleged to have said to Dad: "Do you really think I care what the ambassadors think?" My father replied in so many words that President Roosevelt himself was very much concerned about this wanton bombing and it could be possible that the United States could go to war over this bombing. Von Weichs apparently told Dad he was bluffing. Dad replied that he might be, but if he was wrong Von Weichs might still stop the bombing for humanitarian reasons, but if he was right the German commander could be in for real trouble. Von Weichs is alleged to have said: "Colonel, I recognize a poker player when I see one and I have to say you are a good gambler", whereupon he picked up the phone and ordered the cessation of the bombing.

For this incident Dad was later recommended for the American Congressional Medal of Honor but because we were not at war he received the Distinguished Service Medal instead. However, King Peter of Yugoslavia recognized that he had saved the city of Belgrade and thus the Serbs awarded him their two highest decorations – Karadjordje Star with Swords, third class" and "the

Order of the White Eagle with swords, 4th class."
It is alleged that he is the only foreigner to ever
receive the first decoration.

After he completed the phone call, Von
Weichs asked Dad to sit down and for about three
hours these two professional soldiers discussed the
outcome of the war. Von Weichs tried to show
Dad the invincibility of the German Army and the
vulnerability of the fledgling US forces. He
pointed out that Germany was winning on all
fronts, the U-Boat campaign was bringing Great
Britain to her knees, the Japanese would tie up the
American war effort, and that it would take years
before the United States could rearm and enter the
European conflict.

Dad conceded these arguments but then tried
to convince Von Weichs of the tremendous
industrial capacity of the United States and how
quickly we could mobilize our resources. He
pointed out that Roosevelt had asked for 50,000
airplanes, and that we were laying the keels of
hundreds of warships. He pointed out that the
United States was self sufficient on all strategic
materials except rubber, and had the largest
industrial plant in the world. Von Weichs was not
convinced; however he was also a poker player
and so they ended their discussions with both
placing a 10,000 mark bet on who would win the

war. Wishing each other well, Dad departed and Von Weichs had Dad released and escorted back to Belgrade.

With the German invasion of Yugoslavia complete the German army was now defeating the Greek and British forces further south. Now that Dad was exposed he could no longer roam the country freely because he was a marked man with the 100000 mark price tag on him. His war had passed him by. Hence he and Mother now began packing their remaining household goods and arranging to have them stored until after the war and then shipped back home. (The year before, after the children left, they had sent their first shipment which arrived successfully). This shipment never arrived; Mother and Dad lost most of what they had owned to that date. Most of the things they had brought to Europe with them, and the beautiful things they had acquired while over there, were gone. When they returned they had to buy everything from scratch. It would be several years later, with the help of some thoughtful Representatives, that a special rider to a finance bill was passed in Congress reimbursing Dad in part for his losses.

He left Yugoslavia with a great admiration for the German Army and a complete disgust for the Italian Army. He felt the Italian Fleet was a complete failure that had let down Field Marshal Rommel in North Africa when they refused to come out and take on the British after the Battle of Matapan. Of course in those days we knew very little about the "SS", and about the slaughter of Poles, Jews, and Christian leaders in death camps. Hence his admiration for the German army was purely professional; they had achieved great things with their new thinking.

His greatest admiration was for the Serbs and their willingness to uphold honor over convenience. Many times he pointed this out to me. When Prince Paul was overthrown, even in the face of Hitler's threats, Dad felt that the Serbs were a courageous and stubborn people, and people of the highest principle. He felt afterward that we betrayed Mihailovich because we wanted to keep the friendship of Churchill who had decided to back Tito. He felt we lacked honor; that we had double-crossed those we professed to help because it was politically easy; we had the power to do whatever we wanted but not the moral fortitude. Years later he would admire General Douglas MacArthur's upholding this nation's honor by returning to the Philippines after he had declared to the Philippine Nation that we would return. I cannot even imagine how he would feel today about America's wanton and dishonorable bombing of Belgrade to satisfy the need of an

172

American President for a diversion from his other problems.

To this day Dad never told me how he and Mother got out of Yugoslavia. Mother told us about slipping under the canvas on a barge going up the Danube, and about hiding out for awhile. My sister and brother-in-law later interviewed her on tape (which my sister still has). In that interview she talks about driving up to Romania and finally to Switzerland, but I just don't know how or in what vehicle. His Buick had been abandoned along the river when he entered Hungary. What I conjecture is that Field Marshal Von Weichs must have given them some form of safe passage to Lisbon, for the next we heard of my parents was when we got a call from New York saying they had arrived safely home via the Pan American Clipper from Portugal. The other members of the Legation staff were repatriated through Genoa shortly thereafter.

Before he could rejoin his family in New Orleans, Dad first had to go to the War Department in Washington where he was asked to brief both their staff and that of the White House. He told them what he had found out about the German Panzer organization, and this information was passed immediately to our Armored School at Fort

Knox, KY and to the other service schools. He briefed our intelligence people on Prince Peter's government (now government-in-exile in London), and what he knew of the Greek government-in-exile. He made recommendations for the support of Mihailovitch's Chetniks in the mountains of Yugoslavia and for the Greek resistance fighters. He then went to the Navy Department and briefed it on the Balkan navies and the movements of ships and fleets in the Adriatic. He tried to impress on both the service staffs the importance of the German air arm and its use in supporting ground troops.

Finally, he and Mother got on a train to come back and be reunited with their children and the rest of their families in New Orleans. Dad had two sisters there at the time, and Mother had six of her eight sisters, and two of her brothers there. We had a great family reunion and Dad was the family hero of the moment. Margot and I had to give full reports on all that we had been doing for the past year, how we had made out academically, and all the other things that children report to their parents. Dad was particularly proud of my winning the mathematics prize at the Louisiana "academic Olympics"; certainly this was just recompense for that year in Belgrade where I had to learn algebra by rote, in French.

Shortly after they arrived Hitler launched his attack into the Soviet Union. This resulted in Dad being immediately recalled to Washington where he would serve as one of the advisors to the White House and War Department during those first hectic days of the invasion. While he had no direct contacts to gain information about the Russians, he was still close to many Serbs who were of Russian background or sympathy, and hence he was charged with gleaning whatever information he could from those sources. In December he was assigned the mission of organizing a Joint Intelligence Committee with representation from the War, Navy, Air, State , OSS, and Economic Warfare organizations. This committee was combined with equal British representation to serve the Combined Chiefs of Staff and he was ordered to preside at all Intelligence meetings.

1941 (May-Dec) - Son

The big thrill was in April was when Mother and Dad finally returned to the United States. They had managed to get to Lisbon, Portugal and from there had flown on the Pan-American clipper to LaGuardia in New York. After checking in at the War Department they were able to take a train to New Orleans. Needless to say excitement ran high and we had a big family reunion in New Orleans for which all the relatives turned out. Dad was being written up in such publications as *Time* and the newspapers, and thus was a local celebrity. Tulane University's faculty particularly welcomed Dad home and he was named a distinguished alumnus. Now the stories began to come out about what had happened to him in Belgrade, and so he was besieged by local reporters asking him to tell the "real" story of Belgrade. I think both he and Mother enjoyed the fun. However, it was short lived as Dad then got his next assignment – to Washington, DC. Though our aunts had been marvelous to us, I think both Margot and I were happy to move to Washington and have our own rooms.

In Washington I would learn to drive and become a full-fledged college student, entering

Georgetown University's pre-med course. There my algebra-by-rote background paid off, and my other studies were not too difficult. In fact I was doing very well in pre-med until I ran into the most difficult part; my first encounter with a corpse - actually many corpses. We were summoned to a cold-storage room and there we were shown the bodies that were saved for anatomy study. They were hung up like beef in a cooler, and many were without one limb or another where the doctors had severed the limb to use for the students' study of veins, muscles, etc. For me it was a very unnerving experience and my desire to become a doctor took a severe set back.

There was one course we all loved. It was taught by a Jesuit priest whom we thought was brilliant and we thoroughly enjoyed his classes. He was candid, very open, and a very engaging individual with none of the haughty manner that several other of the priests would often show. It was a course in physics, and he had the ability of all great teachers to make things very clear and simple. He was a natural leader of students. What we did not know then was that he was also a natural leader of men. When war broke out he would sign up to become a Navy chaplain. Father O'Callahan would go on to receive the Congressional Medal of Honor later in the war as the chaplain onboard the *USS Franklin*; a carrier that was severely bombed and damaged by a kamikaze crashing into the ship in 1945. He apparently was throwing 500lb bombs off the deck to keep them from exploding despite flames all around him while directing other men to safety.

We had one other physics professor whose sanity we greatly questioned. This particularly nutty teacher kept talking about "atom power". He stated that one day ships as big as the *Queen Mary* or *Normandie* would use atoms to drive them through the water instead of giant steam engines. Of course in 1941 we thought him quite mad; who ever heard of nuclear energy? He claimed Albert Einstein had figured it all out. He also claimed that time was a variable, not a constant, and that therefore someday we would be able to travel to another galaxy and return. He even predicted that we would, in our lifetime, put people on the moon. As I said, we thought the guy was fascinating but definitely quite mad.

I will never know whether I would have made it at Georgetown and become a doctor. Fortunately for me, and my potential patients, everything changed on December 7th, 1941 when the Japanese bombed Pearl Harbor and we entered the war. At that time the United States Military Academy opened it's doors to additional appointments, and the Army's eye requirements were more relaxed than those of Annapolis. In the Army you did not have to see twenty miles over the horizon, you just had to be able to see 300 yards in front of you. Hence Representative Hale Boggs from New Orleans was prevailed upon to give me an appointment. I was to be the first of his appointments in his long and illustrious career in the House of Representatives. (After his death in an airplane flight in Alaska, his widow Lindy Boggs would replace him and carry on his traditions.)

I believe everyone of my generation can remember where he or she was when they first heard the news of Pearl Harbor. In my case a friend of mine and I had gone to a movie. When we came out the newsboys were hawking papers telling about the attack. We didn't believe them until we got home and found that Dad had left hurriedly (on a Sunday) to go to work. Then we listened in detail to the radio where the attack was described in depth. There was considerable panic in Washington, and of course the radio was broadcasting all kinds of scary things like the fact that soon the Japanese would invade California and capture the Panama Canal.

Mother put us in the car and we drove up Massachusetts avenue to the Japanese embassy. There was smoke coming out of the building, and a heavy guard of US soldiers around it. We were to learn later that the Japanese had spent the better part of Sunday burning their codes and other papers, presuming that we would seize their embassy. We then drove over to Fort Myer which is the home of Arlington Cemetery. For the first time I saw the men of the 3rd Infantry Regiment, who are the ceremonial regiment that conducts all the military funerals and guards the tomb of the Unknown Soldier, all in battle gear instead of their usual formal uniforms. It was an eerie feeling.

The next morning Mother and I went to the Capitol. We could not get in; it was jammed. So we sat on the lawn outside of the Capitol building and listened to President Roosevelt declare December 7th, 1941 as the "day that will live in infamy." The building had been rigged with loud speakers so that his voice, and the subsequent vote to go to war, could be heard outdoors. His speech was very moving and few could doubt that the die was cast, even though, at the time, Mother was disappointed that he did not also declare war on Germany and Italy, the Axis partners of Japan. In a few days that would take place.

We then drove over to the old War Department (the Pentagon had not yet been completed) to see Dad, but he was tied up and could not see us. As I recall it was several days before he returned home to a more or less routine household. However he was very uncommunicative about what was going on. He obviously had read the true reports of the battle damage at Pearl, and these were not very encouraging. They were, of course, classified and so he could not share with his family what had really happened and how badly we had been hurt.

Now the Military Academy took on a whole new meaning. I began to study hard at Georgetown, knowing that I would be going to West Point in the summer. I began to take a whole new interest in things military, and began a serious study of both our Navy and our Army. These would serve me well in later years as I assessed the strategy and tactics of World War II at the Academy and as a junior officer. I began to read in earnest serious books on war, economics, and history. I tried to understand a little about the Japanese culture and its history; these would serve me well in the later years of occupation. Most Americans at that time, including me, were totally unfamiliar with the history of Asia and of the society of Japan. General MacArthur was to be a very unique individual in his ability to understand

and work with the Japanese culture and people. A genius on the battlefield, he was also a true student of Asia and hence a rare phenomenon of a successful occupying general who, to this day, is beloved in Japan.

The year closed with our fighting desperately to hold on to Bataan and to recover from what appeared to be the appalling catastrophe of Pearl Harbor. We knew very little other than that we had lost the bulk of our fleet. It was not until later that we found out that the Japanese had managed to sink our battleships but had not found our two aircraft carriers – both of which were at sea when the attack occurred. These would be crucial in the next few months when the Japanese tried to invade Midway. Interestingly, the Japanese had failed to attack the logistical base of Pearl Harbor – the docks, dry docks, cranes, storage tanks, fuel farm, and repair facilities. Tactically their attack had been a complete success in the numbers of ships and aircraft they had destroyed; logistically it had been a total failure in that it left for Admiral Nimitz (who would soon be appointed to take over as Commander-in-Chief, Pacific) the resources to rebuild and repair the fleet.

The lack of firm knowledge of the true extent of the Pearl Harbor damage, plus the actions of the Japanese submarine that shelled Santa Barbara, and the Japanese landings on Guam and Wake Island created banner headlines of worry and concern. Congress started asking "Why?" and calling for investigations. Suddenly all over Washington one began to see soldiers and seamen in uniform, scurrying from one locale to another. The old Munitions Buildings, (the World War I buildings along Constitution Avenue) which housed the Navy and War Departments were suddenly blocked off, and admission to most public federal buildings was restricted. For about two weeks the City was a rumor factory, and even in our classes at Georgetown we started each day discussing the war. When the pictures of the miniature submarine that had washed ashore in Hawaii, and the stories of the *USS Ward's* earlier attack on a submarine entering Pearl were shown in the papers, speculation was rampant that the Japanese might attack again.

To further the gloom, we began to get reports about the Philippine Islands. The Japanese invasion had gone smoothly; it was only with considerable difficulty that General MacArthur had been able to withdraw his forces on Luzon into the Bataan Penninsula. There, however, they would put up a prolonged and heroic fight before finally backing down to, and having to surrender at, Corregidor. We were simply unable to get supplies or reinforcements to them across the miles of Pacific Ocean and into the harbor of Manilla which the enemy now controlled. Only a few of our submarines were able to actually get into the harbor and get some of the people and the Philippine's gold off Corregidor.

This gloom gripped Washington throughout the winter of 1941-2. It was not until April of 1942, after Doolittle's spectacular bombing raid on Tokyo, that one got the feeling that Washington had settled down into a routine for war, and that the European front once again began to become paramount in the news.

PHOTOGRAPHS

20.   Secretary of War Stimson decorating Colonel Fortier with the DSM. Mrs. Fortier in background in volunteer Red Cross uniform.

21.   General Giraud of the Free French Forces visits the United States. General Fortier served as his aide-de-camp while he was visiting with the President.

22.   President and Mrs. Roosevelt host King George II of Greece on White House lawn. Background in white uniform – General Fortier who served as aide to the King on his U.S. visit.

23.   The author as a new cadet at the United States Military Academy, West Point, N.Y. 1942.

24.   General Fortier prepares for a reconnaissance flight in his L-4 aircraft while on divisional maneuvers, 1943

25.   General Fortier inspects the firing of one of his medium howitzers.

26.   General George S. Patton, Commanding General of the United States Third Army, together with General Fortier, reviews the 94th Division troops in Czechoslovakia at the end of the war. Note other allied officers including the Russians.

22

23

CHAPTER SEVEN

Situation – 1942-1944

Germany: High point of German successes reached in early 1942. Then, in the successive two years, her armies on Eastern front pushed back into Germany by Russian Forces. U-boat campaign finally defeated by Allied navies. German cities suffer heavy bombardment campaign by Royal Air Force and US long range bombers. In June, 1944 Wermacht loses Battle of Normandy and her armies shoved back to Rhine River in the West. At Christmas makes one last counterattack in "Battle of the Bulge", but with its loss is forced back to Rhine.

Italy: Battle of El Alamein won by British; German/Italian forces pushed to Tunisia where they surrender. In 1943 Italy loses Sicily and mainland invaded. Mussolini's government toppled. Allies push way up to the Arno river.

Japan: Successfully seize Luzon, but in naval battles of Coral Sea and Midway Japan's expansion is stopped. US submarine campaign gradually cuts off islands of Japan from supplies from the East Indies. In successive island hopping attacks US forces seize the Central Pacific and gets within bombing range of Japan. MacArthur pushes up New Guinea from where he launches attack on Leyte. In successive naval battles Japanese fleet demolished. Japan resorts to "kamakazi" attacks against US fleet.

Great Britain   Drives Rommel out of North Africa. Assists in capture of Sicily and landings in Italy. Builds up supplies and forces for Normandy invasion. Joint British/US forces land on June 6, 1944 on coast of Normandy and fight to the Rhine River. Moves aggressively against Japanese in China/Burma/India theatre.

USSR: After falling back from initial impact of German invasion, rebuilds its shattered forces with supplies reaching it from the United States. Launches counterattack and in two years of fierce tank battles drives the Germany army from its soil and invades Germany itself.

United States: In these few years the great industrial power of the United States rearmed Great Britain and the USSR, and built a large modern US army, navy, and air force. From this tremendous logistical base merchant and naval ships were created in record time to supply the world and provide the means of projecting US power throughout the Atlantic and Pacific. Landed forces on Guadacanal in the Pacific and on the northwest coast of North Africa in the Atlantic.

1942-1944 - Father

Having returned from Yugoslavia in 1941, Dad was promoted to full colonel and was given the assignment to lecture at the various army service schools and newly formed divisions to tell them about the German army and its concepts of speed and mobility. The American Army was now being formed in earnest, draftees had been called up, the National Guard and Reserve Divisions were placed on active duty, and the United States faced the huge job of training and equipping an army and navy. The key to the Army's success was its service schools, which both developed and taught tactical doctrine. Thus it was imperative that Dad brief these organizations on what we Americans could expect if we were to go to war against the Germans. In addition to his military assignments he was given an honorary doctorate degree from his alma mater, Tulane University, and made many talks to various civic organizations. Thus we saw very little of my father for those first months after his return.

He was also assigned as aide-de-camp to the French General Giraud on his visit to the United States. President Roosevelt was cultivating Giraud as a replacement for General DeGaulle. Charles DeGaulle, as leader of the Free French in London, had always acted imperiously and as a head of state, and expected to be treated as such. He became a very real thorn in the side of both Roosevelt and Churchill. It was said that: "He knew he was God, only God didn't know it". Neither Churchill nor Roosevelt felt he was a head of state as there was no France, and further they had a very difficult time with his personality. It was felt that Giraud, who had been a very popular officer in the French army, might make a better rallying point for the French people. However, after all the political maneuvering, the later decision would be to stick with DeGaulle despite his personality as he seemed to have the greater allegiance of the French.

Serving as aide to Giraud was a pleasant side-trip for Dad. The General was a very likeable Frenchman, with whom Dad could converse to discuss what the French colonies in North Africa might do, and what also the French fleet, some of it in Oran, might also do. These discussions were then reported to the War Department. Dad told me that Giraud was very cautious in his replies, giving the impression that he might not be as well briefed on Vichy France as the Americans had hoped. It soon became obvious that he was trying to straddle the fence between the Free French and the Vichy French. This was what finally got him eliminated from the top job.

Dad also enjoyed serving as aide-de-camp to King George of Greece who came over to give Dad, for his actions in Belgrade, a medal – The Military Cross of the Commander of the Order of George the First of Greece. Of course the King's primary mission was to see and sell Roosevelt on the strategic concepts that he and Churchill had worked out in London about the post war arrangements for Greece in the Balkans. It turned out that we never executed those planned concepts. Inasmuch as King George was a monarch of an allied, though overrun country, he was treated as royalty and given the "grand tour". This included Mount Vernon, New York City, and a visit to the United States Military Academy at West Point where his aide's son happened to be a cadet. (I was given ten minutes with Dad and the King before going back to barracks). Dad did not enjoy his tour with King George as well as he had with General Giraud, because he could speak French with the latter; with the former it was usually through an interpreter.

The visits of the King and General Giraud, as well as the intelligence Dad had gathered, gave Dad a chance to meet with and talk to the President and to meet the Joint Chiefs of Staff and other dignitaries of our government. Though he enjoyed escorting the King around, he told me that he was not enamored of the politics to which he was subjected. He could not wait to return to the field.

Then his own government bestowed upon him the Distinguished Service Medal with a citation that reads: "For exceptionally meritorious and distinguished service in a position of great responsibility as Military Attache at the American Legation, Belgrade, Yugoslavia, in April 1941. Lt. Col. Fortier was charged with the mission of making contact first with the Yugoslav Prime Minister at Zvornik and later with the German authorities in Hungary with a view to ending the bombardment of Belgrade. From April 8th to 12th, Lt. Col. Fortier drove through battle and devastated areas under frequent bombing and aerial machine gun fire and, in order to enter Hungary, traveled on horse, on foot, and on a railroad section handcar through thirty kilometers of the demolished zone. Col. Fortier combined to a marked degree the qualities of diplomat and soldier and by his initiative and prompt and forceful action successfully accomplished his mission and his activities are credited by the American Minister with having resulted in causing the terrific bombardment of Belgrade to be suspended."

191

At this point he was promoted to Brigadier General and appointed the Division Artillery Commander of the reactivated 94th Division. From 1942 to 1944 Dad trained his artillery, conducting experiments for the War Department in six-gun batteries. (Field Artillery batteries of those days in most armies had only four cannon.) The conclusions he came to were that four guns were sufficient to back up the infantry; all the rest of the guns were to be put into what were called "Corps" or "Army" artillery groups, which could be moved around the battlefield to the most critical points.

Throughout all their training Dad continued to lecture his own and other divisions about the German panzer army and dive bomber aerial support. He was convinced that we had to develop the same relationship between the pilots of supporting aircraft and the ground troops that the Germans had achieved. Thus he was instrumental in founding the concept of the "fire support center" which not only developed artillery support for the infantry but also brought in tactical aircraft and naval gunnery support. The eventual strength of the American army was its ability to bring massed fires on the enemy – whether those fires were in the form of artillery, naval guns, or close support aircraft. Lessons learned in World War II would later be applied in our subsequent wars of Korea, Vietnam and Desert Storm. No other army has had better artillery support than did the U.S. Army in Europe in World War II.

The 94th began its training at Fort Custer in Michigan. There the unit underwent first its arming and equipping, then its small unit training, and finally its combined arms training. Custer, and later Camp Phillips, Kansas were encampments and they held little appeal for Mother and my sister Margot who accompanied Dad. Through two cold winters and two hot summers the Division shaped itself, and then finally moved to Tennessee for its final testing. While at McCain Dad was further decorated with several foreign decorations that he had won as a result of his Balkan experience. It was there that the Yugoslav government-in-exile representative brought him his Yugoslav honors.

In 1943 the Division moved to Camp McCain, Mississippi, where it received it latest equipment and conducted intense combat training. Then, in 1944, the 94th Division had passed all its tests and was shipped overseas. They sailed the entire division on the Queen Elizabeth, crossing the Atlantic without escort. It was risky but the high speed of the Queen Elizabeth allowed her to outrun any lurking German U-Boats. After a brief period in England, the 94th was shipped over the beaches to Normandy, coincidently on D+94.

The Division started its war in Brittany containing the German troops in the ports of St. Nazaire and Lorient. Inasmuch as there were approximately 30,000 German troops in each of these two cities, containing them with a 15,000 man division was not easy. The Division was augmented by the French, who, by that time, had put together a division of their own. They also had French resistance fighters, the Maquis, and some additional odd units attached to them. The German mission at the time was to protect these two ports from seizure by Allied Forces, as the use of the submarine pens was vital to Germany's continuing submarine attacks on Allied shipping. It was recognized that we did not have enough force to seize the two ports; so the 94th mission was to keep the cities besieged. There was great fear on the part of the Allied Commanders that the Germans might abandon the ports and use the 60000 troops to attack the American supply lines in the rear.

The Germans had heavily fortified the submarine pens and surrounded them with 88s, the famed anti-aircraft gun of the Germans. They could level those guns and turn them in to conventional artillery, and thus they quickly engaged in counter-battery fire with the 94th Division Artillery. The German were not slow to shoot down our small spotter planes. Hence we had to rely on ground observation to spot fire.

Dad found that the best way to keep the Germans holed up in their ports was to launch continual small unit attacks. Since these could be launched from any sector, the Germans never knew from whence they might be attacked. This gave the Division a lot of practical combat experience without any severe losses. It turned out to be a superb training ground to harden the division for its difficult combat commitments in 1945. These attacks would be launched by individual companies, who would be continuously shuffled around the siege lines. Mobility was the key to keeping these attacks going. Thus did the studying of the Civil War "Battle of the Crater" back at Fort Leavenworth pay off.

At this point the supplies began to run short. The breakout at St.Lo and the rolling of the armies to the East had put a serious crimp in the supply system, particularly artillery shells. We had underestimated how much we would use this arm, and hence had simply not gotten enough artillery ammunition ashore to meet demand. Now Dad found himself trying to conduct small unit attacks, against entrenched German positions, without sufficient artillery to cover his attacking infantry.

Now, suddenly, precision artillery became the order of the day. No targets were to be fired upon unless they could be hit and destroyed with just a few shells. No more rounds would be fired for practice; every shell had to count against a known target.

Rationing was introduced and carefully monitored to insure no waste of ammunition. Fuel also was in short supply but this was not as critical to a besieging division as it was to the armored divisions rolling to the Rhine. It was decided to give this division what it needed to move troops around for the "spoiler" attacks, as it was critical that the German troops not break out and fall on the rear of the American Army heading for the Rhine. Fortunately food, and clothing, supplies were plentiful. The result of these last four months in 1944 was the successful containment of these German troops and their approximately 600 guns which might otherwise have been used on our forces. The Division was off to a most successful start.

1942-1944 - Son

The Academy turned out to be pretty rough on this new-found playboy. In addition to the traditional horrors of "plebe year" (one's freshman year) we were constantly reminded that, since we were at war, if we flunked out of the Academy we immediately became rifle-toting privates in the army. The four-year curriculum was compressed into three years and it was done by simply adding longer academic hours, going to school on Saturday, and studying most of Sunday afternoon. When the school's academic year was up cadets were taken out on field trips to learn about tanks and artillery, or served with line army units to learn a little about practical leadership. Vacations were non-existent our first year, and very short in the following two years. Hence, the three years are a jumble of memories for me but the goal was always clear – to graduate and be commissioned as an officer of the Regular Army.

Cadet life could be quite miserable in those days. "Beast barracks", that first three months when the upperclassmen get a chance to test the meddle of their new cadets, was a nightmare … as it had been for generations of cadets who preceded me. However it did several things for us: it hardened us physically, it taught us the honor system, it taught us the basics of soldiering, and it broke our egos so that we could become disciplined cadets. Of course we learned to march and in the fall would join our companies and march in the many parades for which West Point is famous. We all groused about the "P-rades" as they were then called, but the truth of the matter is that most of us truly enjoyed passing in review in a disciplined formation marching to a very professional band. Our fondest memories are the evening parades that would culminate with the lowering of the American flag and then our marching home to supper. To hear the bugle calls resounding from the mountains that surround the Hudson River as the sun went down behind them was a very moving experience.

Once the academic year started we learned to study in the West Point tradition. At the Academy every class is, in many ways, self-taught. Each cadet reports each day in every subject. One studies the night before, listens to any explanations the officer-instructor might have during the lesson, and then "takes boards" to answer questions or do math problems. Thus one learns to study every subject every day, which, later at Vanderbilt University, would pay off in the six West Pointer graduate-students standing numbers one through six in academic prowess against the other two dozen graduate students. This academic discipline is one reason that the education at West Point can be so comprehensive, and why we could condense four years into three with no decrease in the number or difficulty of subjects that comprised the curriculum.

Another factor that is important to West Point's teaching is the faculty. Unlike the other academies and most academic institutions, the professors at West Point are very few. These are the men who have their advanced degrees and who set and guide the curriculum in their subjects. The actual classroom teacher, however, is a line army officer serving a two to three year tour at the Point. These "teachers", often with combat experience as junior officers, can thus make whatever subject matter one is studying, whether Engineering or English literature, highly relevant to service in the line. Making the subjects relevant to our future careers provided great motivation to study.

We were also graded regularly, and the grades posted in the rank order of achievement in each subject. Thus everybody knew who was making a 3.0 (top grade) and who was making 1.0 (flunking). If egos were bruised that didn't matter; what mattered was that everyone was being constantly judged on performance. This is what happens when one is leading in combat. The troops are always assessing their officers and they will support those they think know their stuff and drag their feet for those they think are incompetent. Thus at the end of each grading period all the cadets would jam the porticos wherein were posted the grade sheets. Then one set new priorities for studying when they knew where they stood.

However, there is more to West Point than just academics. Not that academics doesn't hang over every cadet's life, but even in my day the Academy had a variety of other activities in which one could get involved. For example West Point had a pistol team that I thoroughly enjoyed. Shooting a .45 caliber pistol was a long way from trying to sink little boats with a BB gun. The government-issued pistols themselves were basically pretty inaccurate, so we spent a lot of time honing and tinkering to get them to shoot straight. Once the guns were accurate constant drill was required to turn out an accurate shooter. In those days one used the one-handed, extended arm, method of shooting – as opposed to the two-handed-arms-in front of today. Hence we on the pistol team spent a lot of time walking around holding a book straight out to strengthen our shooting arm. Being a good pistol shot was to pay off for me later when I was in the occupation of Japan.

Physical training was a must and the Academy does an excellent job of getting everyone toughened up. If one was not on a major sport team, you played the same sport in intra-mural. We often thought these "inter-murder" games were even tougher than the major sports teams. I remember my plebe year boxing, wrestling, playing soccer and trying to win for my Company. The most difficult sport of all, however, was trying to manhandle a bunch of whaleboats as we rowed our way up the Hudson River in races. These meets were exhausting. We also fenced, ran track, loped cross country, and ran up the hills that surround West Point carrying a fully loaded field pack. I think we were always physically exhausted, but since that is a characteristic of combat, the training could not have been better.

Athletics did cause one crisis in my life. Time was very short as we raced from one class to another or to the gym. Normally the first thing one did in the morning after reveille formation was to make up our rooms. Sometime during the morning the rooms would be inspected by a tactical officer. Once he had made his inspection we could relax the room standards. Unfortunately, one day I raced from one class back to my room, ascertained that the tactical officer had indeed made his inspection, and proceeded to change into my gym clothes tossing my underwear onto my desk.

Unfortunately that was the day that the Army's Chief of Staff, General George C. Marshall, was showing off West Point to his British counterpart – Lord Ironsides. Needless to say, when the two generals saw my room the Britisher had a wonderful laugh … but I cannot say the same for General Marshall. When I returned from gym I was told to report to a very irate tactical officer who explained to me in great detail what a sorry specimen of a cadet I really was. Fortunately, however, the Chief of the British Imperial Staff was a kindly old gentleman; he persuaded the authorities to "go easy" on me saying he had never before had the privilege of seeing a cadet's drawers hanging from a desk lamp.

Mine was the last class that required horseback riding in our plebe year. The horses were of two types; about one third of them were old nags that had been around the riding hall for many years. The other two thirds were fresh animals just brought in. The joy of getting one of the old nags was that they knew all the commands. All one had to do to ride them was to sit and let the horse do all the work. If the instructor ordered "Fours by the right flank … Ho!" your old horse would turn and fit properly into place without your ever touching the reins. However, if you were so unfortunate as to get one of the remounts, then you had to actually learn to ride and control him.

Hence when the command was given to the cadets to "take horses", there was a stampede to get to the old horses.

One day I was fast enough to win, and so was mounted on a very old nag. I had it made. We went through the hour's drill without a hitch. Unfortunately, at the end of the riding lesson when we were all lined up in a row, I felt my horse gradually sinking beneath me. Shortly I was standing on the ground straddling a very dead animal. The instructor, a major, came by and ordered "Pick up that horse, Mister." I just stood there, dumbfounded, while all my tugging on the reins produced no results. Finally the sergeant rode by and recognized that the horse was dead; he told the instructor and I was dismissed - to a chorus of catcalls from my classmates. I sure was glad when the Army abolished cavalry and went to tanks.

One of the traditions of the Corps of Cadets is what they call the "Long Grey Line". The thinking here is that, from its inception, each year's graduating class joins the long line of those before it – dead or alive. At the alumni parade each June, the returning classes are lined up in the reviewing stand in accordance with their standing. The oldest living graduate stands at the head of the line on the right, the newest graduating class stands at the left end of the line. While we were at West Point during the war, with its restrictions on rail travel, we still managed to always get to the parade ground each year the oldest living graduate. I have forgotten which class he was in but I will never forget the feeling one has about the "Long Grey Line". There is a tremendous sense of continuity to know that once upon a time Robert E. Lee or Stonewall Jackson stood on the same parade ground watching the same review. Some traditions are worth keeping.

One other thing that distinguished West Point in my day was its Honor System. Cheating was simply not tolerated. An officer's word was literally his bond. If one saw one of his classmates cheating or copying another's work, it was an agonizing experience to turn the culprit in to the Honor Committee. However, we did it. We did it to keep our honor intact and to preserve the system. We knew of the many other institutions that had let down their standards or even abolished their systems as "too difficult". To me the knowledge that every one of my classmates was a man of honor meant a lot to me then and ever since. Hence I was to be deeply pained after my graduation by the two honor-system scandals that West Point would undergo in my later years. There can be no compromising on honor. West

Point is the last bastion of that concept and we who were there hold that honor is sacred.

Many years after I graduated from West Point I would have the distinct honor and pleasure of returning there accompanying Mrs. Jean MacArthur, the widow of General of the Army Douglas MacArthur. General MacArthur (and now Jean) are buried in a special Memorial here in Norfolk, Virginia. I have had the pleasure of serving as the Finance Chairman on the Memorial Foundation's board. Twenty five years after General MacArthur had delivered his famous farewell speech to the cadets in, I believe, 1965, Mrs.MacArthur and the Foundation Board were invited back to the Academy to celebrate that speech and to hear a taped version of it once again. To be very candid, this is the way to see West Point. As a cadet my memories are primarily of running up hills, being constantly tired, late night studying, and cold winters. Twenty five years later, going up as a VIP, having the Corps of Cadets pass in review in front of you, and enjoying the hospitality of the Post and its Superintendent … that's the way to see West Point.

The United States Military Academy is a wonderful education, academically, spiritually, physically and practically. The three years passed rapidly and we all matured as men. We learned to live up to West Point's motto of "duty, honor, country". I firmly believe that West Point was the foundation of any success I might have had later in life.

CHAPTER EIGHT

Situation - 1945

Germany:　　　　In May of 1945 surrendered to the combined Allied Armies. Divided into four zones of occupation in both Germany and in the city of Berlin. Hitler committed suicide as Russian troops closed in on the Reichstag.

Japan:　　　　After a continuing series of retreating defeats and naval losses, and suffering heavy bombardment from the air to include two nuclear bombs, surrendered in September, 1945. Immediately occupied by American and British units, was disarmed, and gradually recovered through the benevolent and brilliant leadership of the occupying supreme commander.

Great Britain　　British/Australian forces fought Japanese on the Indus River and gradually cleared the China/Burma/India theatre. With US forces in Europe, drove through Belgium and the Netherlands and defeated the German Army in the north. Was an occupying power in both Europe and Japan.

France　　　　During middle years the French Underground conducted frequent attacks on railroads and supply trains. Upon successful Normandy landings, French government-in-exile returned to French soil. Participated in the occupations of Germany & Berlin.

USSR: Drove into Germany, forced the fall of Berlin, then met with the Allied Forces from the West for Germany's final surrender. Occupied a portion of Germany, Trieste, and Berlin.

United States: After winning the "Battle of the Bulge" and fighting through the "Sigfried Switch", US/British forces reached and crossed the Rhine, drove to the Elbe, and joined with Soviet forces who had taken Berlin. Germany surrendered (VE-Day). US Forces in the Pacific completed conquest of Philippines, and Okinawa before the dropping of the two atomic bombs motivated the Emperor of Japan to surrender (VJ-Day). MacArthur appointed Supreme Allied Commander to conduct Japan's occupation and commence the rebuilding of Japan into a modern nation.

1945 - Father

After the Battle of the Bulge, the 94th was shipped across France to join General Patton's Third U.S. Army. The remainder of General Bradley's Twelfth Army Group was driving to the Rhine, but the Third Army was held up on the Saar and Moselle rivers. Patton gave the job of reducing the Saar-Moselle triangle to the US XXth Corps consisting primarily of the 94th Infantry Division combined with the 10th Armored Division.

The Rhine River runs from Switzerland north to the North Sea, thereby forming a continuous line protecting the German western border. At Koblenz it is joined by the Moselle River which proceeds from southwest to the northeast forming the French border. At Trier the Moselle River is intersected by the Saar River which comes up from the southeast. The two rivers, Moselle and Saar, meeting at Trier, constitute what has become known as "the Saar Moselle Triangle". Here Patton's Third US Army, heading for the Rhine River, was held up by the stubborn German defense behind "dragon's teeth", a series of concrete pillars which had been erected to overturn attacking tanks. The German's called their line the "Siegfried Switch" and dug in behind it; they knew it was imperative that they stop the Third Army from reaching their industrial area.

The line had to be broken by small bits. Thus for six weeks the Division would attack in battalion sized units, supported by the whole Division and attached Artillery. When they had finally fought through the Switch, and the Germans had fallen back on the Saar River, it would take three months of bitter fighting, and cost heavy casualties, before the Division was successful in routing them. The Division managed to clear the "triangle" of German forces and seized the city of Trier. The Germans, knowing the strategic importance of Metz and the triangle, fought with great tenacity. They laid many mines to stop our tanks and booby-trapped everything in sight. Then they were aided by the coldest winter the continent had experienced in this century. Men of the 94th had to fight frostbite, frozen weapons, mud invested foxholes, and the rigors of deadly fighting on frozen ground in which a well-entrenched enemy had most of the benefits. Dad was to tell me of the problems of frozen lubrication of his artillery pieces – they could not be fired until the oil in the recoil mechanisms had been warmed with a blowtorch. The armored tankers found their tanks so cold that to touch the metal without gloves could mean the losing of a finger. It was a vicious, tough, fight, but the

Division accomplished its mission. Many of the dead now lie in the American military cemetery in Luxemburg, the "field of crosses" where General Patton is buried. These were his boys.

The Saar River was steeply banked; there were cliffs all along the opposing side. Where the banks came down to the little towns, the Germans had fortified these gaps with guns and barricades. Expecting this is where a landing force would cross, they insured that no landing force could fight their way into the towns. The solution for the Division was to slip engineers over the river at the bluffs, and have them climb the steep escarpment on the other side, rig pulleys, and at night pull up our tanks, one by one, as we delivered them on rafts. This went on for two days. The Germans in the villages, reassured that no American tanks could get across the river, were totally surprised went a platoon of tanks appeared behind them coming down from the bluffs above. The Germans had no choice but to fall back, and thus allow us to ferry over the remainder of our attacking troops.

Once they had cleared the triangle the Division broke out. Riding the tanks of the 10th Armored, they raced to the Rhine and crossed it at Ludwigshaven. The Germans fought all the way back to the Rhine, but by then they had lost their large unit integrity and so most of the fighting was by platoon or company sized units. They took a last stand at Ludwigshaven, trying to hold the 94th from crossing the river. They strafed the division with their new jets, which had just entered combat. They felt they had to hold ... but they could not. The Division forced its way across the river and then had to conduct hand to hand fighting to clear out the snipers and ambush points midst the rubble of the city.

One of the more delightful duties of a general is to pass out decorations that have been earned by the fighting men. One of the most difficult duties is to write the widows of those that are killed. The 94th Division produced one Medal of Honor winner, 20 Distinguished Service Crosses, approximately 190 Silver Stars, and many Bronze Stars and lesser medals. Dad told me there was no greater pleasure than to be able to decorate one of his men.

It had taken the Division three months and hundreds of casualties, with Division Artillery firing over 200,000 rounds of ammunition, to be able to say "Mission Accomplished". The battlefield performance of both the 94th and 10th Armored Divisions had paid off for Patton's Third Army. Now it was merely a question of rolling through Germany and eventually into Czechoslovakia. There had been fears that the Germans would create a redoubt in the Bavarian sector and hole up to fight on indefinitely. However, once defeated, the Germans surrendered without further guerilla warfare.

Dad's stories of this period all emphasized three things which were paramount in his assessment of the war: (1) the courage of the American GI, (2) the fear of German mines, and (3) the effectiveness of American artillery versus that of the Germans. He felt his infantrymen were brave beyond comparison and even he was amazed at the willingness of his troops both to fight and to endure the bitter cold and hunger. He often remarked to me later that the job of the regular army was to keep the concepts of war intact so as to be able to teach them to the men who would do the actual fighting. These were not the regular army but draftees from across the land, citizen soldiers, who, when the chips were down, were magnificent fighters. He was in actual awe of their dedication.

Originally he had felt no bitterness against the Germans until his vehicles began running over German mines left in the wake of their withdrawal. He always felt mines were a very effective, but cowardly, defensive weapon. He conceded that in desperation the Germans could be forgiven their use. However he felt the booby-trapping of everything as they fell back was not militarily effective and thus was a cruel and inhuman practice that only insured that someone would lose his life or be maimed. He also feared, and his fears would be confirmed later, that as the armies moved on the booby-traps would kill innocent civilians foraging for food or clothing.

Finally He felt that the real strength of the United States Army, besides it tactical aircraft support, was its massed artillery. While we never developed a tank as effective as those of the Germans, or an anti-tank gun to equal the famed German 88, the one thing we did have superior to theirs was our artillery. The ability of the Americans to bring "time on target", i.e. to mass great numbers of guns and have their shells all arrive and explode on the target at the same time, gave us a decided edge on the battlefield. Prisoner after prisoner remarked about the deadly effect of this "time on target."

Years later Dad would add one more reflection on war in a speech he gave when he was Commander in Chief of the Military Order of the World Wars: "The man of battle is also a man of faith. This may not have been the picture of him at home, but all over the battlefield men cluster in prayer. And, I am one who believes that those who did not return are those who had been selected as prepared to meet their God."

As they emerged from Trier, Dad got up one day to find four Germans sleeping not far from his command truck. Drawing his .32 he awoke them and took them prisoner. Afterward, he always said he was just plain dumb and lucky, he hadn't even called for some back up from some of his men. Apparently the press reported the story with headlines "General takes prisoners personally". It received a large press play in New Orleans. Dad felt rather silly about it.

In the spring of 1945, as the Third US Army rolled into Czechoslovakia, Dad received a call from its commander, General Patton, ordering him up to the headquarters. It seems that the Commander of Germany's Army operating in Bavaria was petitioning to surrender but its commanding officer only wanted to negotiate with General Fortier. Needless to say this did not please Patton. Dad asked who this commanding officer was. When he found out that the German field marshal was Von Weichs, the same man with whom he had made a bet in 1941, he told Patton the story and thus Patton authorized him to fly to Von Weichs' headquarters to complete the surrender.

Upon his arrival Marshal Von Weichs greeted him as an old friend and then formally surrendered both his beautiful gold sword and his Luger pistol. Dad initially refused to take the items, but Von Weichs made it clear he wished Dad to have them instead of some MP he would meet later. Von Weichs was well aware of the propensity of the GIs of any army to take home souvenirs. Thus he insisted until Dad agreed. After the formal surrender, the two old soldiers discussed the surrender and reviewed the progress of the war since they had last met. Von Weichs, of course, blamed Hitler for Germany's defeat. Then as Dad turned to leave, Marshal Von Weichs pulled out a 10,000 mark bill – an honorable gesture of an honorable man paying off his debts. Dad was very moved and always considered it the highlight of his military career. Many a family wedding and birthday cake has since been cut with Von Weichs' beautiful sword.

With the war in Europe over, it was now time for Dad to return to the United States. The 94th would later be de-activated and its heritage passed on to another unit in Boston. For all those general officers who had made the tough battle field decisions, particularly those who had spent a life time getting ready to make them, going home was a mixed feelings event. They were certainly happy to be home, and they were very happy that the carnage of war had stopped, but any kind of life thereafter would be anti-climatic.

The first thing that Dad did after he returned to Washington was to requisition from the Army Air Force a C-47 aircraft to fly him to Fort Sill, Oklahoma where his just commissioned son, and his son's classmates, were being trained as artillerymen. Dad elected to take my sister Margot along on the flight, and then to fill the plane with my classmates as he flew back east. Needless to say fifty five years later I still get inquiries from my classmates about "what ever happened to your beautiful sister?" What happened is that she is still beautiful and still my special sweetheart.

This ends the chronology of my father in the ten years that were the apex of his military career, 1936-1945. He would go on to help found the Armed Forces Staff College and the Central Intelligence Agency, and to serve as General MacArthur's deputy Intelligence Chief during the Korean War, after which he retired. In later years he would serve as Louisiana's Deputy Civil

Defense Director, and then be elected to the post of National Commander-in-Chief of the Military Order of the World Wars. But always he remains for me - my Father.

The United States emerged from the Twentieth Century the single greatest economic and military power on the globe with no major enemy as an external threat. Our only threat now lies from within; the forces of anarchy, greed, selfishness, prejudice and abandonment of our God can still destroy us. What have we learned? From my father and those like him who served their country in several wars, I learned that, as in all other things in life, freedom is a gift from God. However, as in all of God's gifts, we must cherish it and preserve it. Freedom that is unable to tame license cannot be defended and will not ultimately stand. Those who do not recognize that our liberty is the gift of a sovereign God will never understand that military might, political cunning, intellectual muscle and technological wizardry offer no safe harbor for the damaged soul. This nation will remain free only as long as we continue "one nation, under God" and be prepared to fight for our honor and principles. The *fields of crosses* of this past century should be our daily reminder of what men of will, under God, can do to earn and keep that freedom.

1945 - Son

For the West Point class of 1945, June was a glorious month. The war in Europe was over, but we new second lieutenants could still fight the Japanese if we finished our branch schooling as officers and got over to the Pacific. Unfortunately, from our point of view, the war with Japan ended too soon. We would not be combatants. The atomic bomb had curtailed our glorious futures as combat officers. However, we would be the first people to land in Japan's occupation and hence the fall of that year was filled with many memorable events.

I landed first at Mishima, Japan, which happened to be the place where Commodore Perry had landed when he opened up Japan to the West a hundred years before. There was still a monument to him in the town. There my artillery battalion would execute its orders to recover and destroy all of the weapons and other equipment of the Japanese army. We would be sent out as teams, headed by a lieutenant, to disarm the occupied area.

When we landed none of us believed that the Japanese would obey the Emperor and not fire a shot, and so we very cautiously started our patrols through the region to gather up and destroy the Japanese army's arms and equipment. My first impression was the same as that described in "Silent Spring", Rachel Carson's book about the effects of pollution on the birds and animals. In Japan, there were no birds or animals. Starving, the Japanese had eaten every cat, dog, and bird they could get their hands on and indeed left the countryside silent. It is eerie not to hear the peep of a bird or the bark of a dog as one enters a village.

As our Jeep pulled into a village we would find it completely deserted. Not a soul or a sound. However, we learned that if we sat quietly in our vehicle in the town center for a while, finally the little children, completely enthralled by an American Jeep, would come out of their houses and approach us. After the first ones had received a candy bar, then more and more would appear. Soon they were followed by very anxious but brave mothers who came to "rescue" their babies from the barbarian invaders. Finally, one or two men would show up. All the adults had been told that the invaders would slaughter them and thus they were very surprised at our friendly attitude. It was pitiful to see what a few cans of C-rations, chocolate from K-rations, or a few cigarettes would mean to these starving but proud people.

The highlight of my military career came a month later, when I accepted the surrender of a composite Special Forces (Kamikaze) Unit. On patrol we had reached an abandoned military secondary airfield where we found a few deserted airplanes and a few Japanese soldiers. My interpreter told me the planes were kamikazes that had returned due to "engine trouble" and the senior Japanese soldier, a sergeant, told us he had been left in charge. When I asked where were his officers he would not answer. Finally, my Nisei interpreter told me to look out over the rice patty. Japanese men and women were bent over their hoes tilling the paddy. He then pointed out four men who were also hoeing but standing straight upright. "There", he said, "are your Samurai officers, for a Samurai does not bend over". Sure enough, when I approached them and called "Attention", they all came to attention and admitted finally they were the officers.

The senior identified himself and then explained that he had some midget submarines in a cove on the coast, about fifteen tanks under camouflage, and some trucks loaded with explosives. His orders had been to stop the US invasion on the beach and he and his command were prepared to do so until the Emperor had ordered that they lay down their arms. He was humiliated by surrendering, but his first duty was to his Emperor, so he surrendered peacefully. I do not believe any of us who saw first hand these defense plans and the Japanese determination to defend their homeland will ever forget President Truman and his gutsy decision to drop the atomic bombs. Moralist today may challenge his decision, but I truly believe he saved literally thousands of lives, both Japanese and American; far more than were killed or maimed by the bombs.

Shortly thereafter the 25th Division Artillery, of which I was a most junior officer, received a new commanding officer. When the new general arrived the officers of the battalion were lined up to meet him, with the colonels at the head of the line and the most junior second lieutenant, myself, at the end. The general walked down the line introducing himself and speaking softly to each of us until he got to the last man. When he heard the name "Fortier" he shouted: "Not Louie's boy ??" The new general was none other than General "Big Red" Colburn, the man whom my father had saved when he was the military attache to Poland in 1939. Throughout the rest of my military career I would be known as "Louie's boy". Knowing my father I deem this to be a great honor.

One of the duties that befell the most junior officer of the battalion was that of Fire Marshal.

The title might sound impressive but the truth of the matter was that the only fire fighting equipment we had was a 1920 Japanese hand-pump truck which, when operating at full capacity, developed a stream of water that would go almost ten feet. One day I got the call that the General's house was on fire. I rushed my little detachment over to fight the fire, but the paper houses of Japan did not last very long in fire. Just as we were about to dive into the fire, out from the smoke strode General Colburn – pajamas pressed neatly, looking just like a general should. He looked at me and asked if everyone was safe and accounted for; I replied that they were, as the only person we thought to be missing was himself. Calmly he looked at me and then casually mentioned that his special hand tooled Czech shotgun he thought might still be in the house. When generals mention to lieutenants "casually" it usually means "do something about it." So into the smoke my sergeant and I went, and fortunately we retrieved the shotgun. When I got out I presented it to the general in a most military way. He took the weapon, checked to see if it was loaded, handed it to his aide-de-camp, and thanked … the sergeant. I won't tell you what my thoughts were at that point. Years later I was to have the pleasure of serving on General Colburn's staff at Fort Sill, Oklahoma. His first remarks to me when I reported for duty were: "By the way, son, thanks for saving my shotgun. I've had the pleasure of shooting many a duck since that day". We went on to become close friends.

I remember the day several Japanese took me out in their boat to shoot seagulls. As I mentioned earlier they had become desperate for food the last year of the war, and thus had killed and eaten everything on shore. Now they were trying to hit seagulls. All they had were old shotguns, I would call them "blunderbusses", with wire wrapped around the barrels, vintage pre-1800s. In any event they had to wait until a seagull landed on the water before they could shoot at it with any hope of hitting it.

At one point a gull circled overhead. I calmly pulled out my .45 pistol, aimed up in the air, pulled the trigger and to everyone's complete surprise, dropped the gull. The Japanese got all excited, tried to get me to shoot some more. For once I was smart enough to know when lady luck was in charge. I calmly blew the smoke from the pistol and returned it to my holster. My thousand to one shot became famous in the region and before I left Japan two years later I met several Japanese who told me about this American officer who, with his forty-five, used to nail seagulls while they were flying. Thus are the legends of history born.

A final event to relate is the earthquake that we experienced. My command, Battery C of the 64th Field Artillery Battalion, had been assigned guard duty in Kobe for the Koshien ordnance depot. This was where a large number of the occupying army's vehicles were stored. The depot lay close to the beach of the Sea of Japan. My junior lieutenant and I had posted the guards that night after which I remained on duty while he repaired somewhere to "have a few drinks". When I returned to our room from inspecting the guard I found him sound asleep.

At about three a.m. the room suddenly shook violently and then shifted first one direction and then the other. All of the furniture slid across the room and back again falling in a jumble. I quickly arose, got dressed and went out to see my guard detail. There were flashes of light all over the city as wires snapped. Near the beach there was not a soul as all the Japanese had fled inland. When I finally found one of them he told me to pull the guards off as the beach would soon be hit with a tidal wave. I did so; just in time. Watching a tidal wave come in, particularly on a dark but moonlit night, is quite an experience. It flooded much of the depot and took out several beach houses. As it receded into the sea it pulled with it some of our equipment and several of our guard towers.

When I got all my men resettled I finally returned to my room. There, lying on the floor under his overturned bed was my lieutenant – sound asleep. With furniture crashing all around him and his bed sliding across the room and back, and then overturning, he managed to sleep through it all. He must have had a monumental hangover when he finally did awaken.

Thus ended a memorable era for both a father and his son. The son went on to enjoy a short military career, build a civilian company, and have the delight of marrying his wonderful first wife, Maureen, who, while she lived, was his inspiration and the mother of his five children. Then, after her death, God gave him a second wonderful wife ... but all that's another era and another story.

The End

CITATIONS

(1) James C. Humes, *The Wit & Wisdom of Winston Churchill,* p.117

(2) Humes: Ibid, p. 119

(3) Humes: Ibid p.123

(4) Collection of private Fortier letters in author's possession.

(5) Private letters: Ibid

(6) Private letters: Ibid

(7) Ray Brock: *From the Land of the Silent People",* p.6

(8) Leigh White: *The Long Balkan Night,* p. 207

(9) Arthur Bliss Lane: <u>Life</u> Magazine, Fall 1941, p.103, article entitled *Conquest in Yugoslavia.*

(10) White: OpCit, p. 222

(11) Cecil B. Brown: <u>Saturday Evening Post</u>, April 23, 1941 article entitled *The Germans are Coming.*

(12) White: OpCit, p.241

(13)   White: Ibid p.245

(14)   William E. Crawford: <u>Boys Today</u>, October 1943, article entitled *The Man Who Saved Belgrade"*

Photographs courtesy United States Army Signal Corps or from author's private family collection.

Cover: Image Arts of Birmingham, Alabama

ISBN 141200046-7